The Wing Collection

By the same author:

The Wing Collection: New & Selected Poems

Diane Fahey

*For Angela,
with kindest thoughts, and my love,
Diane*

PUNCHER & WATTMANN

First published in 2011
Published by Puncher and Wattmann
PO Box 441
Glebe NSW 2037

http://www.puncherandwattmann.com

puncherandwattmann@bigpond.com

National Library of Australia
Cataloguing-in-Publication entry:

Fahey, Diane

The Wing Collection: New & Selected Poems

ISBN   9781921450259

I. Title.

A821.3

Cover design by Matthew Holt

Printed by McPhersons Printing Group

This project has been assisted by the Australian Government through the Australia Council, its arts funding and advisory body.

Contents

Small Wonders

The Wing Collection

The Gold Honeycomb

The Sixth Swan

Secret Lives

The World as Poem

small wonders

Terns

who fly epic arcs, slipping through
atmospheres, past sleeping continents –
so good at bathing, too: cajoling brine
over wings with shivering leaps backwards
then a final shimmy ten feet above
as if to baptise their former selves.
Next, the charisma of flight – their bodies
such an ingenious fit with the world
as they side-swipe the wind, ride its back
to reconnoitre the river, make lightning-culls
from the hearts of sudden white flowers.
Later they stand, dumpy yet winsome
on mirror sand, facing out to sea:
their eyes calm, gleaming like homely stars.

Air

The hem of a magician's mantle flaps;
from a stand of trees, one tree crown lifts,
leaves fling outwards, grow swiftly into
a host of ibis wings. Borne, trance-like,
on tideless waves, they bathe in summer air,
trail silhouettes across the sun – now
a caravan in a desert of clouds,
now the skyline of a mirage city; on wild days,
the wind's anarchy made visible.
With their beaks and wing-tips, bodies of light,
they forge cambered paths, sculpt valleys, cliffs,
shape live holograms that encode worlds,
hold in shadowless, eye-tricking tension:
breaking apart, coming together.

Solo

Every feint and nuance that humans know
faced with the well-armed onslaughts of others
is present in the flight of this small gull:
a suavely parried climb becomes a slide
sideways down a wind that would douse it
in melted pewter — but for the panic-swift save
as wings cut a piece of sky, rise clear:
a jagged graph of strength reclaimed.

Now it coasts with a confidence won from
uncertainty, the wind's power its own.
This, the one bird at the estuary,
foregrounds miles of ocean when it swoops low:
capping tiered green with an abstract flourish,
scaling vertiginous whiteness.

At the Cliffs

I'd hoped for a marsh harrier, keeping
its place in the wind — a bookmark between
airy pages — or some voyager from
Antarctica, in its white glide the carved
silence of ice. My gaze hovers, sweeps along
that crack in the sea: a fault-line of foam,
jagged as a gull's flight through storm.

The rip tracks shorewards, past where surfers
skate and bounce along glass arcades,
skidding down as snowy paws clamber
towards the rock-shelf — beyond which the dunes,
fragile haunt of the red-cap, ascend through
marram reefs to these cliffs: laced with gale-blown
shell grit; algae; the bones of birds and fish.

Albatrosses

You look down at them from the cliffs: a pair
traversing oceans of icy air – their wing-moves,
climbing or gliding, as simple-subtle
as a dialogue of speech with silence,
the stroking of a beloved into deep calm.
Whiteness ribbons above waves spitting and
swallowing white, swilling shards of sea-glass
that catch the sun's unwatchable eye.

Awe turns envy towards aspiration:
to be as actively at ease in life
as they are in flight; to let essence flower
wildly and truthfully into time;
one's life a gracile imaginary line
drawn through the measurelessness of things.

The Parliament of Birds

Clouds airbrushed on aluminium;
peat-brown shadows of scrub — these hardly stir
as a kelp gull glides over its image,
lands with a card trick of wings; an egret tracks
a quartet of diving black cormorants;
the heron peers from its harlequined patch.

On the mudflat, ibis and moorhens feed.
Swans delve offshore, remoulding their shapes,
or float upstream with glacial smoothness,
able to move through opposites, at will.
The river is a still mind but for bird thoughts
that probe the depths, or splutter upwards — like these swans,
whose white-fringed wings now chequer searchlights
beamed through golden rips in cloud.

Pelicans

Where the river becomes a lake, a descent,
majestic and unassuming, onto
sheet lightning: with benign ease, the fleet
water-brakes, foam smooths to glass beneath
a marriage of power and tranquility.
Set in ivory discs, irises
are ancient coins worn to a sliver, fusing
sun and moon, each with its secret door.

Their gaze holds the stark acuity
of the voiceless. Pilgrims more than predators
they seem, but scoop from shoals with bladdered bills
pink as baby ears, as their own egg-selves —
growing wings that will be hollow-boned,
snug beak-prong, puffy eyelids like goggles.

What Herons Know

Ascending from mudflat to cypress
the herons veer between straight line and curve
as miraculous wings contend
with their own heft. Perched in green twilight
each wears its body like a disguise:
a retired wizard, perhaps — behind that
shadowy gaze, a lifetime of shape-changing —
or an old philosopher culling
minnow-truths by day, to be relished
in this half-heaven. Mellow croaks speak of
instinct tempered by time. Real ecstasy,
they know, waits inside the long stillness —
or sweeps in with winds that solve puzzles
on the stream's surface, offer new ones.

The Ibis Grove

Riverside, six Monterey cypresses
rise from a garden, their wolf-ear tufts thatching
a tenement of branches. Each evening
ibis fly in: as they settle, an opera of
hooked rasps and drawn-out croaks, till night comes down.
From the pier I watch an estuary
flat as a tarn, but for the poetry
of surface tension, embossing a white sky,
the drowned green tower reaching towards me.
Beneath it, later, the coming dusk
already inside that creepered cavern,
I hear the wind-crack and jarred groan of a ship
tacking beneath clouds the stained white
of ibis plumage, miming their dusty cries.

Owl

This poem starts in a tree hole where,
caught by a cuckoo-camera, fuzzy frights
shriek their need. Eyes closed, I see thick night,
a barque with sumptuously ribboned sails.
Superlatives, a few, must be invoked –
the most soundless feathers, the sharpest hearing
(those ear-slits, points of a Bermuda triangle).
And the eyes? – mortal lamps to hang fables,
new omens on; the descending lights
of *glaukopis*, 'the shining-eyed one'.
Who does not long, somewhere in themselves,
for the embrace of cataclysms of softness;
to be met by that startled, eldritch gaze
searching the furthest corners of their soul?

Wedge-Tailed Eagle

Then I saw for the first time over these fields —
the sky a padded ceiling, miles of light
seeping from the sun's wound — those hypnotic
swerves, a mark of dominion like all else:
its height, its eight-foot span, its primeval
patience.
        It turned, an archer's bow;
became a bold emblem that could impress
the red seal on a document of war;
rip out an eye.
        Heaped in baroque abundance,
its wings, though, were operatic — their soaring
like a voice in rapt accord with silence,
yielding itself to, and enfolded by,
light: empyrean at last.

Tawny Frogmouths

I saw three of the ugliest creatures my eyes had ever beheld. They were Tawny Frogmouths, about half grown and with scraggy necks outstretched, big eyes and mouths agape showing the hideous yellow of the inner mouth and throat like big ugly goannas, fit subjects for any nightmare indeed.
— P. J. Wood, Geelong's Birdlife in Retrospect

Gateway Moonah Park, Barwon Heads, is home to a pair of tawny frogmouths.

I search for the tree that can look back at me
from streaky grey bark: twig-lidded eyes
at first blearily half-closed — human eyes
full of grouchy surmise — then yokes in eclipse,
suspended in syrup; brooches of jet-
on-gold, pinned to fur lapels. At night
plumed crowbars wrench into flight;
by day, bough stubs pose in cryptic stillness.

Classic outsiders — sack of a body,
weak legs, as ugly as sin — they dream of
a *trompe-l'oeil* fusion with wood. Under threat,
rat-trap mouths chant 'OM' with steely truculence,
a door swings wide on a chamber lined with
pus and jaundice, a thousand failed sunrises.

Lyrebirds

At Healesville Sanctuary

It is achieved, done with: inside the bark walls
of a broken tree, a female broods an egg
cupped in grey feathers plucked from her flanks.
He's out in these fenced-in, ferny acres
performing to attract a new mate –
who never will appear. A vaudeville mimic
of ambulance and firetruck, camera-click,
chainsaw, staple-gun; and of his peers:
grating shrieks of the black-cockatoos,
cries of bowerbird and the kookaburra,
his favourite – sometimes a whole party
giving their upbeat answer to life.
His tails fans out, a silver canopy;
now for a fresh run-through of the repertoire.

Cockatoos at Dawn

In eucalypt crowns beyond the lake,
large white petals emanating light –
some, as the wind whips up, flow in drifts
from one home-tree to another: unwreathed
then garlanding themselves anew.
Soon, the day's migrations will begin,
sparse handfuls or noisy clouds of them
rowing with careless strength through winter-gold
that x-rays the wings of low fliers,
a buff glow to match the moon's rice-paper;
their crests, sleek compacts of question marks;
their voices, reedy and tremulous –
childhood melded with old age; their speech
gaudily innocent of words.

Macaws

So this is what parrots become
when they let themselves go,
allow excess to roost in their souls —

breasts in sunglasses-strength saffron;
blue wings an untidy archive of
noon to first star; old-jewellery-box

tarnish on ragged wedding train...
Huddled in nit-picking love
they touch beak-coloured tongues;

drape swathes of plumage against
each other; in amplified propinquity,
air pinions twitchy as radar.

Jesters more than saints, yet
at times a piercing probity,
the hint of immutable intentions.

Near dusk, a royal progress from perch
to sequestered cage — mobile bric-a-brac
colonising a Victorian parlour

with shrieks that could wake the dead,
or scold them back to sleep:
this gorgeous waddling into the dark,

the light on their feathers undressed by it,
zebra-lidded eyes noting you,
the exotic, without condescension;

wisely adapted, fantastically sane,
lacking only a rainforest.

Small Wonders

Superb Fairy Wrens

Portly, brash, they seem
small essays in certainty;
engage nest-thieves in
'song-battles', send them packing.
Otherwise, sweet-voiced, gorgeous.

Splendid Fairy Wren

Head-on: monocle-
sized. His mating costume is
purple, cornflower-blue.
In eclipse: sober brown, wings
tinged with turquoise – a promise.

Lovely Fairy Wren

He's made a career
out of blue; now, songs to guard
young, call to confreres,
his mate... valiant ascents
laced with fallible pauses.

Variegated Fairy Wrens

But for upright tail,
mauve-blue, matching his, she's plain.
With lavender breast,
hyacinth head and chestnut
epaulettes, he lives in hope.

Zebra Finches

Her decor's restful,
buff, fawn-grey. He wears neck stripes,
spots, rouged ear patches –
hints of jungle, and circus.
In common: wax-red eyes, beak.

Silvereyes

Plump, precision-built,
yet somehow subliminal –
movements faster than
thought; white-ringed, heart-of-dartboard
eyes hypnotise then vanish.

New Holland Honeyeaters

inhabit, become
jasmine and rosebush, taking
just what they need; sing
floriated canons; leave
in an excitement of wings.

Budgerigars

Faces, sun-yellow;
bodies, leaf-green; discreet beaks,
small eyes... they're warmly,
dazzlingly, unassuming.
Outback flocks rise, block the sun.

The Hummingbird Suite

Hummingbirds

Surgeon's-probe beak, wings
bolstered by their own down draught;
on ghostly whirrs of
speed they hover, shunt backwards,
sideways, drinking throat to throat.

Hummingbird Colours

A moneyed sparkle
on emerald-indigo;
violet ears; throats
of ruby, cobalt. Their blooms
of choice: red, sun-orange, pink.

Hummingbird Statistics

Some near-weightless with
three hundred breaths, one thousand
heart-beats, per minute;
eighty wing-beats per second;
nest, small as a halved walnut.

The Humming Cage

Caught, fed nectar, killed.
Their skins and feathers adorned
the Aztec kings; were
talismans of strength, and hope,
god-like might, beauty of heart.

Hummingbird Feathers

On a shaman's cloak
their power lives on: myriad
wings pollinating
bee balm and *mariposa*
in sunlit, vanished forests.

Hummingbird Mysteries

Torpor occurs nocturnally for most hummingbird species.

They glow at will, die
temporarily each night.
Resurrection takes
an hour, transfiguration's
glory a nanosecond.

Hummingbird Dreams

To be held aloft
while drinking the world's nectar.
To be on the wing
yet still. To create phantom
wing-shapes in the air, that sing.

The Mating of Hummingbirds

More a matter of
spirit than body; swifter
than time; a brilliant
but not quite plausible trope
penned by a spellbound poet.

Male Swordbilled Hummingbirds

With bills longer than
their bodies — the Cyrano
de Bergerac of
hummers — they clash, parry, thrust:
rapiers propelled by wings.

Hummingbird Sustenance

Tiny winds scatter
glorioles of gnats. Always
hours away from death
they drink their own weight daily
with grooved, lascivious tongues.

Bee Hummingbird

At two grams, the smallest hummingbird.

Hard to imagine:
the tongue-tip hairs that assist
the theft of nectar
from bells, trumpets, chandeliers —
beyond a thousand each day.

Albino Hummingbirds

Moth-like, sun-starred wraiths
poised high in air, or sipping
from voluble flowers
among shouting choirs of leaves,
their wing-sound a muted breath.

Hummingbird Questions

His Speech was like the Push
Of numerous Humming Birds at once
From a superior Bush –

– Emily Dickinson

Each hushed syllable
of wind equals how many
hummingbirds, rising
from salvia, phlox, larkspur?
(A vocal ambrosia.)

Hummingbird Soul

As for death
I can't wait to be the hummingbird,
can you?
– Mary Oliver

Every cell nourished
from wells of sweetness; a wise,
yet questing, presence,
uplifted by the dazzle
of vividly witty wings.

Humming

A meadow of bees;
mother with child; musician
in thrall to silence;
and these veiled wings blurring
hearts of flowers – work-song, love-song.

In Praise of Seahorses

Each luminous yellow eye
   scans a different view,
      reads forwards or backwards.
   Head and body belong in profile:
heraldic seal, carven knight.
   It hovers in cameoflage
      near tentacles of eelgrass —
   that coiled signature-flourish
an anchor as it feeds.
   A hummingbird-blur of fins
      fuels its stately progress,
   ascent and fall.
Miniature selves
   belly into life from the male —
      custodian; enforcer of liberty —
   pouch pressed against a whelk:
conundrums of tails and snouts,
   a wake of possibilities.
      Through manifold
   appearances it moves:
fluorescent pink,
   bottle-green,
      black-spotted,
   tangerine — this is:
hippocampus,
   cavalluccio marino,
      le cheval marin,
   das seepferdchen,
the seahorse.

Weedy Seadragons

With something of a race-horse's
        vigilance of eye,
                taut slenderness,
        they move just faster than
the speed of stagnation –
        by drift, out of
                sheer necessity –
        sip plankton through a straw,
sport manes of kelp
        that ripple like tourney flags
                as they flow nowhere –
        at one with their milieu.
(How we know the slippery
        veils we hide amongst.)
                Flares of mauve and gold
        help them stay unseen...
Light fills a weightless body
        found, sea-stripped,
                near sandy feet.
        Ants circle eye-sockets,
work at a final cleansing:
        this innocent bone
                patched with fish-skin,
        its shape rhythmed
in an upbeat –
        a gracefully complicated
                wave, poised between
        quietism and
a quirky valour.

Leafy Seadragons

Too formless to be heraldic,
in quite the wrong element to breathe fire,
hoard golden piles, these dragons
are dreaming they are plants.

Mobile, sprouting reefs,
they've let themselves run to seed and leaf;
even in a world of flotsam
they are oddballs, pariahs...

Up here, translated, a lot would be
artistic types – cast far-out boundaries in bronze;
as body-sculptures, cross the line between
animal and vegetable.

In a world of mirrors, round eyes
would grow more quizzical still,
acquire a patina of sadness.

Some would become eccentrics,
cultivate an unkempt look –
in despair of being loved for their true selves.

The extroverts would write to newspapers –
barbed, off-centre letters;

the introverts brood morbidly
on their sex lives, send for chest-expanders,
built-up shoes, hairpieces.

But, at Carnival-time, all can be
otherwise.
            This one, for instance,
rides high on a float, beside
a woman dressed only in diamonds.

She smiles starrily at the crowds
then smoulderingly at him:
Aphrodite to his Hermes.

He's no spectre-with-eyebrows, now,
but life's other principle:
beside Desire – unchanging,
ever-hungry as the sea –

he is the chameleon self
in its fulfilment:
the one who knows he does not know
what he can be, who he was, or is –
shape-shifter; multiple question mark.

And, far from that glitter,
he is the one who – humble among
the weeds – becomes the image
he contemplates;

who can create surprise
while ever an adept of patience:
'Wait and see,' his tender counsel
to the unembellished young.

Wolf-Fish

The mouth a seal of sour violence,
clamped down on what refusals?

An armoury of fangs – each year
a new crop grown – needs only

the knowledge culled by the eye
afloat in its celluloid bubble.

Once harvested, beheaded
in the name of happy marketing

lest shoppers be unnerved by
an odious look, or suddenly falter –

teeth tearing into flesh built from
sea urchins – remembering

pressure's slow fuse, sight
a shadowy filter, the grinding

of stone into dust to reach
smudged tears of meat.

Hate feeds on such small morsels.

Starfish

Some loll in corners, in recovery from
louche lifestyles. Others, draped on stones,
image a wise passivity: five-point
mystics practise the art of stillness, ponder
the enigma, *As above, so below*.
Arms of yellow, buff-pink, peep from ledges
or frankly overlay one another.
In the most intimate embrace of all,
gourmets cloak prawn or crab, kidnapped oyster –
each back a sensuously rippled sea.
Travellers glide, ghost-like, on swirling tubes.
Those time fails become blue jelly
on the rock shelf nourished, shaped by, breakers:
a maze of water gardens inlaid with starfish.

Pearly Nautilus

A dweller in far depths
    it moves through ocean's
        full harmonic range,
            glides under a ceiling
                on which the night sky floats.
Inside miles of silence
    it seals chamber after chamber
        with mother-of-pearl walls,
            grows outwards, linked by
                a thread to the centre.
From it I take an image
    for Mozart's music,
        each intricate, sculpted
            whorl, the datum of
                a prodigious unfolding –
mind-in-flesh
    building, bequeathing,
        this abstract iridescence:
            a moon-curved wave
                ascending time's spiral.

Dragonfly

Navigator of the winds,
       cartographer of translucent maps,
negotiating all angles, planes,
       with dreamy precision.
Such creative flair
       in each switch
from headlong surge
       to hover;
from loftiness
       to sparkling descent.
What terrain does it chart?
       Freedom, and freedom's limits:
unmeasured choices
       within elusive bounds
as the field of force shifts
       sideways, clockwise.
A nebulous world
       builds swiftly in this
shimmering garden
       on a breezy afternoon.
To trace the dragonfly's path
       with a thread of cobweb
would be to wreathe and stitch
       lime trees, roses, dandelions
together, crazily,
       in an ecstasy of invention.
Or, point to point,
       connect all dots…
Would that produce
       a veined pattern on air's
diaphanous membrane
       like the wings of a dragonfly?

Cicadas

Holes pock the ground;
husks cling to stucco,
spine the lilac trunk;

in a whirr of cellophane
small zeppelins veer up
towards the tops of trees.

Sometimes their song
is a razor-strop rasp
back and forth

over the mind,
at others, patience
in tension with longing.

In mid-spring
their climbing voices
promise heat, sex, death —

an iridescent throb
like a benign nerve;
an image beyond reach

provoking memory.
Befriending me,
one covers cheek,

nose, an earlobe,
with ticklish tracks,
invades my hair.

Three amber gems
stud the velvet between
its eyes — so mildly red.

Close-up, I see the light
they hold, pupils
small as poppy-seeds,

then lift the cicada
back to earth and slip indoors –
enveloped still

by that high-pitched
chant, once nurtured
at the roots.

Late Summer Garden

The butterflies make no sound, seem always
to be travelling away from sight.

Copper and alabaster keys
they have the freedom of the garden.

One quivers like a nerve
against my thumb's blue base: its wings

ragged and veined, pressed like petals
between clear leaves of air.

What nectar has sustained
that forthright orange, chameleon brown?

A dust of pollen radiates from where
the wings, almost unhinged, touch the body

haloed in dark hair. The eyes of the wings
have opened and closed a million times.

Air quickens, drifts the butterfly down
into grass sewn with yellowed leaves,

and buttercups − glossy, unfading suns.
Above, the bright fluttering green

of trees that have breathed and sung
with all the strength of summer.

Red Admirals in Shropshire

Borne one after another into the high white room
the butterflies would keep me from writing poetry.

Flames rimmed with jet, they flicker against rafters, glass —
as if flight could take their bodies anywhere.

Some, tiring, raise wings under-patterned with bark.
Once cupped, released, they sheer away with pent-up speed,

one paired with another freed moments before,
to trace a mutual, tottering path

through air with no glass veils, white cages.
By evening, room and hillside hold no sign of them;

the last of summer is a balm resting on eyes and skin;
my hands remember their dry flutterings.

Butterflies: a Meditation

1
The poem's creation:
a flight path seemingly
without pattern,
bewildering to the naked eye;
at moments
an incomprehensible lightness.

2
The poem itself
                is a wing:
a taut membrane
that radiates colours
beyond human sight.

Its eye, always open,
startles – can command
your gaze, track you
through any kind of darkness.

3
At a distance, ethereal.
Nearer, their wings, all texture,
invite a close reading

of scent-scales, hairs:
some, laminated
to create iridescence –

a shimmer the eye
cannot photograph.
                Poetry again...

4

The legendary Blue Xerces is gone —
grasped at by many hands.

Clear-wings know the ways of light
too well to be possessed.

Between these opposites
all butterflies hover:

poems pinned between pages;
dream-bearers sent by gods.

5

Among the hydrangeas;
on elder-flower, prunus leaf —

beauty exists always in relation:
mates with its mirror-image,

stores reflections of itself
in glass palaces,

skirts the edges of vision —
a blur of coral, lobelia, salt-white.

6

What will these leonine wings
connect with, where alight?

Metaphor is such a dance of
possibility, a weightless touching:

Leaves of bronzed gold on
yellow buddleia, late sun.

7

The butterfly as psyche
that lives in the body, the poem;
inhabits the flesh of words;
feeds us images of ourselves;
plants us deeper inside
now, this.

8

But the body, after all,
is pivot of flight,
storer of fuel,
centre;
the journey
a line of energy
unravelled from it.

So poetry moves —
in arcs, at tangents,
an instinctive
map
around ordered
garden, wilderness,
ocean, the great globe.

9

Poems with poison in them
flaunt themselves — why not? —
pose as invincible.

More-vulnerable others
blend carefully with background,
stay intransigently what they are.

10

The poet as lepidopterist:
not the laying on of hands
but the laying out of wings.

11
Butterflies sup on
nectar, honeydew and sap;
carrion and excrement.

Poetry, too, sustains
itself on sweetness,
and on what is most rejected.

A city of petals
flutters above dung.

12
Always this doubleness:

a void that breaks down structure,
draws in despair;

a fallowness by which things
grow into themselves,

patience the alchemy –
spirit bodies, weavers of light,

shaped in a darkness
sealed by transparency.

Monarch Butterfly

Devouring the fluted transparent dome
from which it came, then milkweed –
sequestering toxins against predation;
becoming a tigerish tube, intimate
with the opacity of green.

Sealed now in a crystal womb that grew
inside caterpillar skin, it remakes itself:
imaginal buds convert each cell
till webbed patterns press through film
studded with glints of golden rain.

In darkness, a sudden tearing, the body
making its descent, pumping blood
to straighten wings that will fly it
across continents, in a host
masking the sun, shrouding conifers

with fragments of stained glass, a baroque lichen,
burnt-orange leaves that will outlast winter.
The return to origins is in a relay
of generations – an imprint of memory
indelible as black veins.

I look down at a curated flame
bereft of the third dimension. Nearby,
the viceroy's counterfeit – innocent of poison,
incapable of epics, yet a brilliant rival
flaunting its stolen immunity.

Ego, alter ego, they co-exist,
each a singleness in multiplicity,
as still as they were wont to be in life
when about to fly off, or having just alighted
on an afternoon drenched with pollen.

Moths

Soft, almost unseeing sentinels,
they wait without purpose on walls,
in cupboards, ready to be disembodied,
like candle flames, by a finger-pinch.

As cupped hands open to outer air,
they fidget, cling — do they know
how to be saved? Some prefer
to grow brittle on curtains, silk fringes.

Yet, multiplying as if by thought,
they have their future strategies:
pupae wreathed inside lids, buff wrigglers
chiselling rice to webbed clumps.

Most are radiantly nondescript,
somewhere between a sheen
and a colour; others, bark paintings:
a geometric opulence.

Tonight, one climbs the shadow
of the lamp, flirts with
the twisted gold nerve that draws
dull mysteries to fulfilment.

Bees

Bees, then.
I haven't thought of you

for months, except when
pegging out the clothes,

feet shifting
in clover where you work.

Pollen bearers
who serve fertility,

you are the ones
I've most wished to celebrate:

guardians of this hive —
building and humming,

storing and culling —
the shapers who know

the ways of the queen-muse
with her gorgeous abundance,

the sterility she inflicts
as she lies being nurtured.

Do you remember
the golden honeycomb

of Daedalus,
the twinned-bees brooch

from Knossos,
Mycenae's beehive tombs?

You dance through these images
of opulence, ceremonious

balance, death;
there at the birth of poets,

buzzing and swarming
near the mouth

to instil
the gift of eloquence.

Your own voice declares
a pitch of knowledge,

expresses
your life's music,

provides the ground bass
for other voices.

In close-up,
daemonically hairy,

you are a transformer,
part of the bedrock of things.

Bee Flies

Of bee flies, little is known
which suits them well.
They begin life by imposing on others —
locust, velvet ant, caterpillar.

Hairy impersonators, they wear
a long proboscis, have perfected
a nimble, darting flight,
frequent flowers.

If their bluff is called
they have no sting,
preferring to go unarmed.

The non-conformists among them
disguise themselves as wasps
(in lower case, of course).

Subtly persuasive they may be,
but what is finesse
against the thugs of this world?

Mere common criminals, robber flies
catch them on the wing —
to be bound with spiny legs,
punctured, devoured...

Better to end by evoking
their glorious moments —
how they confused the ancients
by milling like bees from carcases;
from the honeycomb, death.

Earwigs

Provenance of name unknown – lost in
some entomologist's periwig, or fallen
from his ear-trumpet into an inkwell.

When needed one could always be found
in manuscripts, combing the fine print,
leaving, if squashed, a messy signature.

Unlettered bibliophiles, earwigs can feel
secure between the most unnerving thoughts,
subversive quips; are untroubled equally

by the pedestrian and the soaring.
Endowed with wings rarely used, pincers
slow to take the point, they fare best

in the great outdoors, investigating
yellowed pages of Brussels sprouts,
promoting life's general raggedness.

To hold or behold them may not be pleasant
yet they are quite unexceptionable –
forked tails curled up in meaningless threat.

Should they create a society, build
cities of fragments, promenade their young,
we might find them interesting, or endearing.

But what they like is to bore small holes in things.
Still, they know patience, make devoted mothers:
woven, as we are, into the world's substance.

Cockroach

Blackly armoured as a dictator's funeral,
arch-survivor so easily crushed with my foot,
you die as you lived, without expression,
squat body, fine carapace, fusing or sundering.

I know a further million of you wait —
the underground sea on which this house floats.
While I was gone, you tracked each plate, pot, cup,
dining on the ghosts of past meals; invaded
sealed crates of books, a ghostlier sustenance.

Moving with the illusion of slowness
then cannily absent, you often subvert, outwit.
Sometimes, I find you in dreams, or odd pockets
of the self — just there as if to say:
> *I cannot be transformed, kill me or endure me.*
> *Remember, nothing describes me but what I am.*
> *And don't write poems about me.*

Mosquito

What if *you* could move freely through darkness
with the ability to miss all slapping hands –
wouldn't you make that continuous raspberry sound,
blowing your own trumpet, slicing through
wakefulness, sleep, dream?

Only when pausing to drink is it defeated.
Dracula requires a stake through the heart by daybreak –
the mosquito, one self-punishing swipe
bringing it back to visibility:
a smudge of ash on blood.

Millipede at an Ashram

Utterly free of mind
it attains the centre
of the meditating circle,

begins a series of
yoga asanas,
curving, contracting –

that pliable form
adopting with ease
the postures we strain for.

At rest, it turns
inwards – a black coil
with silvered spine.

One of us not yet touched by
enlightenment,
flings it out the window.

We stare into a hollow
core of space, remember
to keep breathing...

On a sunlit leaf
the millipede nibbles,
does nothing.

Grasshopper

Arrived somehow indoors.
Minute but well-armoured,
with battledress skin,
matchstick thighs
steely with power.

In a time warp
it vanishes, appears
an arm's length away –
mind, and eye, unable
to track the image.

In the grass-green carpet
of the meditation room
it loses itself, enacts
the leap of stillness:

spirit lightening flesh,
flesh grounding spirit.

The open doorway casts
a grid of honeyed sunlight;
the garden pulses, unfurls.

Midges

Mere nothings-in-particular
pocking windscreens on hot, booming days;
over long stretches of half-rain
curved smears beneath a wiper.

Or a host of them whirling past headlights,
their harmless darkness
utterly seen through
as they dance
towards sea-drenched wastes...

Us they affect only by chance,
and we barely impinge upon them —
with our hard shells, parting
their delicate dust-storms;
nudging a drift of air;
crystal flash in a moonless night.

Fireflies

Happy the tree
illumined by candles, warm stars...

A host of airborne lights
turn on and off
in concert –
seeking attention,
inviting interest.

From unseen branches
a green brightness flashes back:
she knows, she's watching.

Gradually,
lights disappear from the tree –
the brilliant collective
lost in the humble ceremony.

Now the makers of light
revel in its absence.

The cosmic tree
silhouettes itself against
the many darknesses,
waits for dawn
as it waited for night.

Mayfly

A shape in the depths
filtering, feeding,

inventing new versions
till the pale template

of completion rises
to break the surface,

fly to the water's edge —
there to emerge

in its final image.
A few hours or days left.

From a glistening cloud
the downward flutter

of a mating; myriad eggs
threaded to a stream-bed.

Fluted wings at rest —
mazes of crystal veins

sealed by sunlight, as if
aeons ago, by amber.

the wing collection

Dürer's *The Little Owl*

Set down by the faithful hand
　　　　of Albrecht in 1508:
　　　　　　　your feathers, crisp and reticent
　　　　　　　　　as young leaves;

claws, so carefully askew
　　　　in the delicate geometry of nature –
　　　　　　　holding on to a world,
　　　　　　　　　holding back from a world;

eyes, brighter than an hourglass,
　　　　as alive as hearts
　　　　　　　yet more full of darkness
　　　　　　　　　than a forest.

To each of us you seem
　　　　a true, unspoken self
　　　　　　　forever hidden from
　　　　　　　　　life's puzzlement.

In fragile, jaunty babyhood,
　　　　you outlast the fall of forests,
　　　　　　　watching in wakeful dream
　　　　　　　　　who learnt your life in darkness:

a creature – a simple, single world –
　　　　alive again on fresh parchment,
　　　　　　　beneath the warm, empyrean touch
　　　　　　　　　of Dürer's brush, in 1508.

Sparrows

The Venerable Bede spoke of
the human soul as a sparrow flying in
from encompassing darkness
to pass through the bright hallowedness
of a sanctuary, then out again...

How often I have seen them —
hopping briskly, never out of place —
in the neon smog of the Underground;
or usefully pecking spilt grain
in the temple-ceilinged supermarket,
its blaze shrinking daylight to a shadow.

It seems, in any kind of shelter
they will try to find a home, however
makeshift, or unhallowed.
If one could send the Venerable Bede a letter,
one might offer the information that

here, now, darkness is often disguised
as light; and that, grounded from free flight,
many learn to survive in the bounty
of simplest things, planting a creaturely
presence in bare, unfavoured nests;
small candles open to every wind of night.

Wings

At the Art Museum of Basel

Angels with eagle wings, intricate
as fugues, set to scythe eternity,
but empty robes – each swirling fall
flicked upwards by light winds.

Artists who painted them had bodies
inside their robes, and wings
visible only to the eyes
of posterity.

Saints, hovering in between –
some barbaric in armour:
the daemonic divine...
                    ('Oh Lord,
preserve us from the wrath of Thy saints!')

Still others, vulnerable as reeds,
laid waste by their ardour,
wait with eyes brimming before
light's wafer, the gift of peace.

Brushes, wing-tips:
how the gold of vision endures –
humility and hope steadfast, bonding
these haloed figures in earth
as they turn, with the gravity of sunflowers,
towards an unseen zenith.

The Annunciation

After Fra Angelico's painting in the Museo de San Marco

The long stone corridor ends at Savonarola's cell
lined with portraits of his dark-boned face, eyes
of fire and cinder, that muscular mouth whose words
drained the bloom from Botticelli's faces,
leaving them to parch inside an airless gloom.

You walk back past the chaste twilight of each cell,
peer at figures in robes bloodied, or filled with light —
each one, a masterpiece for the inward eye —
you walk back until you reach the starting point
where you see again the girl who sits, unstartled,
on a bench, quietly admitting the angel to her thoughts.

He is plainly there, his wings methodical rainbows
of yellow, crimson, blue; between halo and wing-tip
he spans an arch. He has come to announce, to gaze...
Hers is the stranger face. Her skin, free from
Byzantium's gold, wears the warm clear light of Florence.

In garments of primrose, olive, she leans forwards,
listening. The angel waits on her word which she gives,
and it becomes flesh. The light does not change.
Only her folded hands tremble. There is no other sign.

She is the one about whom we have imagined everything,
know nothing. 'This joy, that grief, were what Mary felt
when her son was born to her, lost to her, tortured, put to death' —
litanies of tenderness, apocrypha of pain,
we have invented to comfort, punish, ourselves.

She has been given, in recompense, a sinless life,
virgin motherhood, a death without corruption,
and an assumption into clouds of rose-tinted gold.
She asked for none of these. She asked for nothing:

                                        'Thy will be done.'

The cameras flash but do not illumine her eyes,
opaque and shining as drops on a blade of grass
reflecting the white and gold of the small flowers,

                                the scarlet of a passing wing.

Angels: a Dossier

Apparitions

At dawn, a figure looms
from horizon to zenith,
a heaven-lit shadow
above burning coals;

a gyre of wings, faces,
blindingly bright,
rings the meridian sun —
a golden whirlwind;

high over the cliffs
a bird-like form
hangs on a thermal,
outlined by will-o'-the-wisp light;

inside eerie brilliances
of cloud and lightning,
for a split second
a flame-shaped presence.

Visitations

Embodied, they come amongst us,
feet almost touching earth,
the hems of their robes
twitching for take-off,

their rapt, attentive faces
not quite human
never less than perfect.

Messengers who cannot be killed,
they bring omens, good news;
with monastic calm announce

the seeding, saving moment:
       the depth of the Divine
       illumining a fertile soul.

In bare-floored studios —
dust motes drifting through ladders of light —
they lend their eyes to artists, poets,

guide laden brush or nib towards
incandescence,

ensure each rhythmic row of feathers
glows coral red, maize yellow,
ocean blue;

damascene haloes, wing-tips,
so they'll shimmer in candlelight.

Guardian Angels

       a benign shadowing
       a prophetic vigilance
       a timeless listening
       an enfolding otherness…

So palpably invisible
you know they must be there:

beings of light
       who spark the soul's intelligence,
       summon leaps of faith,
       sow patience.

They do not need to breathe
but sometimes do,
in sympathy.

They have no cause to feel
but often do: standing close
they allow tides of grief
to pass through them;

act as bulwarks against
gale-force passions,
the virus of wanting everything.

> On a dawn cliff top, they hover
> in the half-smile shared by strangers
> as a vast wing of sea light
> spreads over feathery darkness.

Shoulder Angels

The one on the left, wearing
crimson tights, promises the world,
probes with his pitchfork for hidden desires,
sports a prehensile tail
able to wrap around your mind.

Aureoled by electrum,
his counterpart, in snowy alb,
meditates on your right shoulder,
sending into your soul's bloodstream
a thirst for peace,
> for the balm of its completeness —

> an airy nudge:
> > *eternity now*
> > *eternity now*

Icons

1

Tobias and the Angel, Workshop of Andrea del Verrocchio

Verrocchio gives us an older brother,
buoyantly strong, who walks beside
Tobias with a dancer's step.

Raphael – soon to reel in
the story's next silvery twist;
reveal the healing secret –
shares the glory of his wings'
palette with his charge:

whose amaranth-hosed legs
in umber boots, plant him
so convincingly on earth;
whose black and lapis lazuli cloak
lifts, swirls, would fly.

2

Jacob's Dream, Rembrandt van Rijn

Jacob sleeps beneath a canopy of care:
the half-sketched watcher
holds out his hand, palm down –
instilling the dream
with a look of such grave compassion
as to make the angelic seem
an enhanced humanness.

3

The Annunciation, Jan Van Eyck

Arrrayed in an archbishop's
traceried gold cope —
deep-slitted at the back
so tinctured wings can slip through —
Gabriel waits on Mary's words
with the graced stillness of one
able to move between spheres
as effortlessly as a singer's voice
travels from one window to another
across a summer courtyard.

Praise

On this planet
where some few can engrave —
with pulse slowed, breath held — a poem
onto a human hair

on this planet
the size of a sunspot —
an outrush from one of the sun's pores,
an open furnace door

on this planet
whose every plant and creature
seeks fullness of being —
a poignant efflorescence —

we cannot hear those choirs that praise,
under the cathedral light of heaven,
the Source, the Mystery,
which holds us all in life

yet catch echoes of their frequencies
in sacred music here,
                    rising like incense
from chapel, mosque and temple,
from grasslands, rainforest, desert.

A holy hearkening.
                    The sound of radiance.

Flyers

On Alain Tanner's film, Light Years Away

Daedalus

Daedalus, with a furrowed wizard's face,
squints over plans, adjusts his desk lamp in the hangar.

The wings take shape, a cut-and-paste job, basically –
though the birds, with their screams and their lime

lend the idea some holding power,
a kind of credibility.

In a glimmering void, beaked faces
fringe the drawing board.

Adversary

But the freshest eagle will undo the dream –
brought down so grievously, from such a height.

All tragedies are irreversible; his, unredeemable:
claw-eyed, he means not to be upstaged.

Departure

Feathers of paper, bones of tin;
the scratched goggles that will not suffice;
and promises of another meeting,
'light years away' – where else?

Offstage, the flight begins;
the youth gathers the birds with broken necks,
remembering... between strapped wings,
that bloody wrinkled breast:

('It's their souls' power I need –
son, try to understand.')
                              But one has escaped
to argue the case, and flies – an unbroken arrow
held dead on course by the scent of blood.

Apprentice

He finds him, a wing-trapped bundle in a field.
From those pecked-out wells, he – Icarus – once drank deep.

A mere two hundred miles – write it off as a brave pittance.

Yet something within has changed, so that the young man sees,
without imagining, the point the wizard aimed for,
the place from where, horn-beaked, he now looks down.

Birdcage

Crows with sensibilities like aqualungs
thrive in the murkier regions of the cage.
Fledgling sparrows flex their wings,
aiming for the highest perch.
Upon dead branches that move beneath them:
pigeons, who love town halls, monuments;
and parrots, of brazen eye but limited vocabulary.
Blackbirds with bitter, darting looks
see it all and keep their cool. Peacocks parade
their imaginary lawn, the floor.
On wooden bars, finches
and budgerigars gaze. A swift beats wildly
against the roof. Canaries twitter,
watch the crows. An eagle with broken wing
sweeps with visionary eyes
the darkness between bird bodies.

Doll Writer

The warmest skin tone to be had, outside of
being alive; an expression, sweetly grave,
that puts the best possible face on things.

Her eyes hold starlight, deep-sea dark;
in their *millefiore* fixity
a concentration that cannot falter.

As the message comes through, her guided pen
trails copperplate – the angelic script,
spider-web fine. With seamless hesitancy

a verse – well-turned, heartening to those
with heart – takes shape on the moon-white page.
She does not recall accident site; fire;

the paralysed girl in the attic –
has no dreams of fall and dismemberment,
the fashioning of a brave composure.

Garbed in green silk, the sewing needle's shine
still upon it, she sits at a gilt table.
Were the prime mover large enough, she could write

volumes – multiple tongues and mouths
voicing thoughts from a depthless font.
It's as if a dancer on a musical box

had been translated to a chair, seduced
to language: haunted by lost cadences
her letters trace lifting arcs, loop downwards –

earth-yoked, while feeling heaven's pull.
Glassed in, she breathes rare dust: mirrored by
paperweight eyes, peach cheeks, bud lips.

Remembering Ophelia

1
Blood trickles down from the castle,
filling the flowers that fill her eyes.

2
Confused, and the victim of confusion...
How water clarifies the mind.

3
As they lay, littering the hall,
her spirit lingered among
crumbling masonry and pillars,
in weeds and flowers
intermarrying outside the walls.

4
Centuries later, she returned with a film crew.
She was wearing jeans, an Indian shirt
embroidered with flowers.

He was still lying among the others,
with their sprawling limbs and broken swords.

After the filming, she took off her badge,
pinned it to his chest – *TAKE THE TOYS
FROM THE BOYS*, it read – then left
without a farewell kiss,

though she was compassionate,
and over the bitterness by now.

5

He wasn't mad, because he knew he was mad.
She was mad because she didn't.
That was why *he* knew when he was dying,
but *she* didn't.
                    Did she know he wasn't mad?
No, because she couldn't.
                    Did he know she was mad?
'Madam, I never think of such things!'

6

Invisible rape —
he had penetrated and withdrawn
without laying a finger on her.
You wouldn't find it
in any statute book.

It made her think
the real thing must be awful.

Sometimes, she laughed and cried for hours
but mostly, there was her sewing now;
and she fiddled a lot with her shawl.

7

He died surrounded by enemies
who were really friends
who were really enemies... *et cetera.*

She died alone.
But on the hillside were hedges
full of scrolled leaves, birds' eyes
and knots of wood — all watching.

8

The rats were leaving the castle,
grey drops sliding down escarpments —
prelude to some final loneliness.

9

She was surprised when they asked her
to do the flowers for the funeral — such an outsider
in her bare small plot against the wall.

It was a grand State Funeral,
of course, with a huge monument
plumb in the middle of consecrated ground.

She decided on violets, daisies, rue —
all her old favourites.
Strange, he had never liked flowers.

'Such frail things,' he'd winced,
'so ephemeral, so easily crushed...
Like you,' he'd added, with a sneer.

'Oh, we're all mortal,' she'd replied,
'and anyway, *I'm* not afraid of ghosts!'
(She could stand up to him in those days.)

How apt her words.
Death had come for them both, soon after;
and, now that she was a ghost,

and saw how natural it was,
knew she'd been perfectly right
not to be frightened.

10

How could Ophelia,
still in the mermaid state, drown?
On a bank of the river she combed her hair,
refreshed after her swim.

A fisherman passing by
conceived an immortal love for her.
Merciful, she gave him a smile,
a big warm kiss, and sent him home.

11

She could remember him much younger,
muscular chest and loins straining
through leather as he whispered,
'God, Ophelia, you're a real turn-on!'

Her Mum had said, 'Keep your distance
for a while.' Then, with a seasoned smile,
'Don't worry – he'll get over it!'

Next, he had gone away to College;
and come back. ('A real *hinterlectewal*,'
sneered her Dad.)

One day, she met him in the High Street.
There was a long silence.
She said, 'Funny world, isn't it?'
'Rotten,' he said, and walked on.

'He's just not interested,' she thought,
'just as I'm getting to be,
with all those fantasies of kissing
and fondling, and swimming
naked in the river.'

12

'It's not polite to leave the world without saying goodbye!'
That's what they told her on the Other Side, and sent her back.
These days she's a florist in Kensington. She knows the world
a little better this time round, is almost ready to say hello.

Primal Scene

The summons comes at a late hour — so inconvenient:
she's propped against pillows, glass of port to hand,
reading *The Case of the Disappearing Doppelgänger.*

A night journey. Soon after eight, she trudges up the drive,
refuses tea, strides to the summerhouse. Suddenly,
she's staring down at a vacant space, shaped like a body.

No proof of crime yet, but where has this life disappeared to?
By nine, they've assembled — the whole jittery cast:
over dark crescent moons, stunned eyes avoid each other.

She paces the room, tests each angle and point of view.
That tired woman on the sofa, where's she in all this?
And the girl with bitten nails, a desperate smile.

By the aspidistra, duster in hand, the spruce maid.
(That costume's clearly a facade.)
                                    She herself is in drag
on this occasion — crossed boundaries can disconcert,

help cut to the truth; besides, the best thinking's done
in a collar and tie, so they say. Using her watch as
an *aide-mémoire*, she starts the questions...

Life as a Freudian detective story! What can't, or won't,
they remember? What did her in, made her fade clear away?
Who holds the key? Will any clues be found?

At one point, a child had run across the room —
plump, with dark curls, an unfrilled dress. Whom did she cling to,
look away from? Quick, write it down before it's lost!

The time has come for her to stand in that void
outlined on the floor, stare everyone hard in the eye,
say something eccentric, then leave.

Return to Start: She travels back through the labyrinth
to where the book lies open on the coverlet;
under her bedside lamp, the port glints...

      'Nine a.m. They're assembled in the summerhouse.
      It's Sunday, the air outside balmy –
      a trampoline for bees. Inside, humidity.

      They watch me circle, then enter,
      that mummy-shaped form.
      This is the optimum moment.

      If there's to be a revelation,
      it must come *now*...
                  I turn slowly,
      meet each pair of eyes –

      all blue-green, like my own.
      After a tortuous silence
      an unexpected voice begins to speak.'

From *The Mystery of Rosa Morland*

Seamus L'Estrange: Spirit Photographer

Not for me, the charades of revenants —
women, robed in lurid grey, their eyes
hypnotic, the dark gleam of effigies
risen into life from carved stone tombs —

nor the dead child, dressed in Sunday best,
grafted back onto parents fixed by
grief's dissolving stare — an uncanny
double, anchored near head or womb.

Once, though, in a derelict house, as I
photographed a stairway leading nowhere,
midwinter noon bloomed from an unseen source,
and — the cloud of dust I'd stirred up, was it? —

a glimmering shroud hung in icy air;
I yearned to walk through those ghostly steps.
Thereafter I sought light-effects
that fused the unearthly with the human —

accidental poltergeists of brilliance:
a cypress avenue, corridored by summer,
to which a blown mist brought metamorphosis;
candlelit rooms of cigarette-fuelled talk;

a forgotten kettle boiling into
sunlight — all yielded chimerical
glimpses, my lens positioned itself,
the shutter guillotined illusion.

I saw, where rock sliced a waterfall,
figures dancing above white tumult;
an avalanche rolled ice into sea foam
alive with the unborn, the unretrieved.

Stranded by storm, I watched moon-drops touch
and traverse a windowed darkness – making, of absence,
a continuous presence. My gaze plumbed
that fathomless transparency.

At this moment, I sit staring at light
through my sealed eyelids: particles
of jet and gold mingling; glass shadows
wreathed inside a mandorla;

a mural on a great dome
pulsing with my invisible blood.

Walpurgisnacht

Walpurgisnacht doesn't concern Englishmen.
  — Jonathan Harker, in Bram Stoker's Dracula

After we drove through the peasants with their clogs and alpine teeth
and eerie whisperings, ('Walpurgisnacht'), the coachman doubled our speed.
The sound he uttered was voiceless — a ghost sound: *Wal-purg-is-nacht.*
I savoured the word, quaffed its vertiginous brandy,
then lapsed back among cushions: I do enjoy my travel.

Our coach was hurtling down the profile of a mountain, the valley steaming
like pitch, a sky empty of sunlight. Increasingly at ease
I tried to chat with the driver — now almost incoherent,
his English quite gone. My German, though, was fast improving:
'Walpurgisnacht!' — that fall of syllables so pleased me,

I conjured a Hotel Walpurgisnacht, even a restaurant of that name:
(*What would it serve?*) By this, we had entered the valley's maze,
night upon us, the horses emitting high-pitched screams —
the driver, too. I felt ready for a nap. When I awoke,
much refreshed, the rattling wheels and creaking sway of the carriage

were my only points of sensory reference.
I sank deeper into burgundy plush, lit a cigar —
its molten tip the one visible spark in creation.
What happened next, I can't recall. The story told is that,
the coach having overturned, I was extracted from it

by a wolf-like being which slavered, undid my necktie, and...
Just then, soldiers arrived and doughtily fought off the creature
which slunk back to the woods, or graveyard, or wherever
it had come from — perhaps that odd-looking inn over there?
Under a heaven of lanterns, fear-glazed eyes trawled my neck, found it pristine.

90

Though shaken, I was still in good spirits and richly enjoying
the atmosphere of the place, drinking it in for future use:
branches thrashing and breaking, unholy cries, stigmata-rain...
On my return, the Royal Society asked me to lecture;
though I've always been one for dispelling myths about

foreign parts, I declined. For you see, the writing bug
had bitten and I was in a mad rush to get it all down.
This was, let me tell you, the happy dawn of my long
(and dare I say, prestigious?) career as a Gothic novelist.
At my desk, words have flowed seamlessly —

except for that slip with a paperknife: fortunately,
my powers of self-healing are remarkable, wounds leave no scars.
Oh yes, I've got the temperament for the writing game.
Quill into ink — the neat, sharp beauty of it!
For me, a deeply gratifying way of life.

'*Red* ink?' rasped my publisher when he saw the first manuscript.
'For God's sake, Clive,' I said, 'allow me *one* eccentricity.'
Beyond that, I've not explained: couldn't be sure he'd understand...
As before, I keep in touch; each week, it's up to Town:
dinner and cards at the Club, a stroll in Pall Mall.

I never leave home at full moon, though. I so love
the look of the garden lying drenched in a carnage of silver blood
as I wander the grounds, hover by nooks and ivied bowers —
or stand at the highest window, in formal evening clothes,
commanding the whole scene: my monocle flashing,
                              my lips in a thorny smile.

Dracula

The coil and hiss of his cloak
streaming through high windows
like a black curtain.

The bed is curtained in white
and billows like a ship.
Appleflesh! *Just a tiny toothful,*
he tells himself. She falls limp
on her pillow, matching its pale.

He is left in the wind-filled,
corniced room, satisfied
but lonely.

Assignation

Some inner light shines through the cracks
in his teeth: 'Velcome to Transylvania!'
(at least, that's what she *thinks* he says –
his accent is rather thick.)

A dusty room with a dustier feather bed
is given her at this gingerbread inn.
The woodwork is highly wormed,
but interesting.

The hotelier winks with his seeing eye,
knowing she is the adventurous kind.
At eleven, sure enough, she exits through
large cracks in the shutters, slides

down the hill and up to the castle,
where he is waiting. He serves champagne –
the best – then smiles, his teeth pointed,
with many cracks. She smiles too,

her neck in a brace from that ski fall
in Sun Valley when, even so, she'd finished
and won the race. Her teeth are regular,
like all Americans', and seem to fill the room.

She unwinds the crimson scarf. Her opponent's eyes
blur for a moment, then focus.
'Chess?' he suggests, bravely. He knows
he's in for a long and lonely night.

Last Scene

*...sometimes he himself, who feared that if I lost track of him I should despair
and die, left some mark to guide me. The snows descended on my head, and I saw
the print of his huge step on the white plain.*
— *Mary Shelley's Frankenstein*

Always, at the back of my eyes,
I saw my pursuer. An intemperate peak
showed me wild gashes tracked by tooth-prints —
small clean bites of them, till they meshed with
a new rhythm, flailing towards chaos:
the death of a mind, its every device
and delusion, an embellishment on snow.

At last, alone. Even in that unbounded place
I felt in myself a vastness, imagined
whale inside iceburg, as I staggered towards
sea-line, thirsting for a frozen magnificence,
to be preserved inside a tower that could
travel oceans, slice ships, buckle ice floes —
an island where no tern lands.

Assemblage

I wake, reposition my head carefully
back on my shoulders, revolve the bolt.
Dents in the teapot on my breakfast-tray evoke
the dimples, oily with light, I'll dive into at the pool,
a liquid bowling green draining through shark gills.

I wear a twenties' costume – black wool, knee to neck –
but anyone can see my skin's rough patchwork;
that my joints have metal accessories.
I am what I appear to be – a walking industrial accident.
Thirsty for reassurance, I lope to the spa:

the circle widens with distant looks, its temperature rises.
'O, that this too too solid...' But no!
Resolute fingers clamp bubbling thighs, I check my toes.
Back in the change room, I fiddle with scar cremes,
anti-rust spray, busy as a drag queen.

A half-fogged mirror shows two eyes, almost level,
almost equally blue, in this botched, transparent face
that will never tan. I'm an artefact, I know,
yet some kind of human – I can think with halting
fluency, admire sunsets, want love.

At home, the mirror is edged with cloud-stains –
a *fin-de-siècle* lithograph. Diving through deep-sea eyes,
I ask: *How much is retrievable, how much yet unborn?*
then turn away – terminally bemused, of course,
yet also quickened, scenting an animal peace.

The Collector

Would it be the turkey-feathered pair? – the most convincing,
after all, while 'mysteriously uplifting,
possessed of shamanic power,' (so read the label) – or these

made from opaline discs, with their seraphic glitter?
As he adjusts the lights, water lily pads of silver,
kingfisher-blue, and damask, float over the ceiling.

But for old-fashioned comfort, why not 'The Greenbacks',
thick with dollar bills? How reassuringly they rustle
as he flaps his arms: perfect for when the market is rocky,

a deal hangs in the balance... The small 'Eros Wings' next –
their feathers synthetic, yes, but expertly copied
from a Titian painting; a bow and quiver accompanied.

He yawns, steps past 'The Leonardos' – too contrived!
Yet 'The Dream of Icarus' stops him. All the more authentic,
claimed his Guide at the Wing Salon, for being spliced with wax

and a relic of Antique glue. The feathers? – wedge-tailed eagle.
He'd spent so freely they'd offered a bonus: 'Garden Wings',
made of leaves 'microwaved to remove all moisture, insect life';

they dazzled in their demise – paper-thin skins of apricot,
plum, guava, each grafted into a sycamore twig.
'Ecologically sound, these wings can be recycled:

draped over compost, they'll revert to earth, roots, leaves,
may therefore become more "Garden Wings".' In theory,
admirable... But tonight, sporting red silk pyjamas,

he craves 'The Overlord'. Hoisting black leather
pinions onto his back, he grasps the matching whip
and watches that Mephistophelian shadow

trying to stare him down. Whistling and jeering, too,
like a football hooligan. No class at all! Anyway, what's the joke?
He flicks the lash — a studded snake rears in the mirror.

The harness is heavy but he's strong, will stand waiting
that phantom out till he has won: can let pinnacled wings
crash him to the floor, lie amongst them in dreamless trance.

Litany

the lilies of the field —
Can they add value to the Dollar, erase the Deficit?
  Will they buy me a Maserati, or a Beach House?
   Could you open a Bank Account with one?

the lilies of the field —
Of what use were they when I sought
  Contacts in High Places,
   Special Handshakes,
    a Leg up the Ladder?

the lilies of the field —
After I'd reached the Top
  why didn't they save me
   from Boardroom Rivals
    plotting to bring me down?

the lilies of the field —
What solace could they offer
  when my life turned against itself
   & Emptiness devoured me?

the lilies of the field —
Cut them down, root them out.
  Let them be shipped off
   & sold for funeral wreaths;
    crammed into gilt vases
   as backdrops for the lily-white smiles
  of Politicians, Captains of Industry
& Media Moguls, in all their Glory.

the lilies of the field —
Plough up the land where they grew
  & spray it with poison —
   spray it again & again.

the lilies of the field —
They were clueless about defending themselves
    & now they don't exist —
        so there!

the lilies of the field —
Relax, forget them.
    You've won.
        What's next?

Sower

On Jean Giono's The Man Who Planted Trees

Most change is slow, tries not to happen:
as with seeds, for instance, which half-ask
to be mislaid, mixed up with stones,
give birth to life twisting back on itself,
as the parable warns, and promises.

With hope, without expectation,
a man buries acorns in a hillside –
serving the dream, free to forget them
as he hollows and fills; each one,
a few minutes of his life, no more.

After, he sees the rain in a new way,
feels the sun's heat entering earth
as it enters his flesh. When he is old
there are oak groves. But not for gods
to fill with prophetic voices,

or for humankind to possess
by so much as a glance.
They are for themselves –
axis of heartwood; leaves,
transforming without speech,

powerless to bear messages from
the gods, withstand human encroachment.
Oak tree after oak tree:
all, in their sacred green moment
shared with jay, warbler, mistle thrush, owl.

the gold honeycomb

Philomela

In flight, but hardly
swift enough...

Her limbs splayed,
bruisings to the marrow.

As if in afterthought
he cuts her tongue —

this man of flesh,
this man of blood.

Days — shadows
flickering on a wall — pass.

At last it comes:
the healing gift

she has waited for,
summoned in lost words.

So now she rises on wings,
feels, almost, peace;

then hears the song — her own,
that she could never sing —

and, yes, is reconciled:
in the song, free,

and in flight, always
swift enough.

Scylla, Daughter of Nisus

At what moment – wrapped in
  the sea's leaden cloak –
    did she begin to imagine
      breathing water?
   In that moment
  her body transformed;
the wings she first thought
  fins, began to move
    so that she spiralled upwards –
      a slow, unbreathing climb –
   then broke through the waves'
  winged surge to circle higher,
tranced by surprise,
  the escape into sunlit air
   a radiant pain.
     In such an altered body
   she knew a different world –
  without longing, joy,
but with their perfect expression.
  Close-by, kindred sea birds
   tended their nests.
     Cold winds blew,
   ruffling the down of
  the newly hatched, claiming
their most hidden warmth.

Niobe

At the end, what bird could you have become?
One that can never return to its plundered nest
and must circle and circle until it falls –
only in death accepting any resting place.

But as stone that can weep, it will take
immeasurably longer for you to wear yourself away:
the grieving commensurate with the loss;
that slow trickle down flesh as cold as the gods.

Andromache

Heroes widow their wives, who must embrace paradox:

After he left, I was with him all the time;
his every ache, deprivation, I felt before he did.

When the messenger came, I told *him* the news;
only the details of death needed to be named.

Now they drift through our home like flakes of ash
or buzz like slow flies around my head.

Sunlight invades each room, shadows the hearth;
somewhere, a storm splinters the air.

The house is utterly empty, it is thronging with presences;
weeping, I cannot hear my voice, which is everywhere.

After a hero closes his eyes, they keep him awake forever;
when I close my eyes, I see the years I have lived –

a felled avenue of trees; I see the years ahead –
dark birds watching me, circling me, giving me

more and more time.

Hecabe

If this darkness that I am in,
that I have become,
had a voice,
what would it say?

That grief turned me inside out
and still more came...
Being no longer myself
I could not bear more
and mirrored back to my enemy
his cruelty to me.

When he murdered my son
I felt he'd taken me inside
a room filled with clawing hands
and blinded me.
So that's what I had done to him.

Now we are both childless,
in darkness: he, cursing me,
swiping with broken nails
at whoever comes near,
and I, wondering
what else I could have done.

When the violated become
the violators,
what gods will hear them,
to whom do they belong?

Astyanax

1

Victory yields a new set of enemies:
   the homeless, the defenceless, the small –
    including this child
   whose birthright's the bravery of his dead father,
   whose inheritance is a ruined city.

2

Odysseus decrees that Astyanax, 'Prince of the City',
be flung from the walls of Troy.

The messenger warns Andromache:
'If you protest, he will be left unburied.'

3

But Andromache is silent,
contemplating the changes to come:
   mother to childless woman,
   widow to concubine,
   citizen to alien,
   aristocrat to slave.

4

Astyanax, who took fright at the horsehair plume
of his father's helmet, is placed in Hector's shield,
his broken body recomposed; seed in a pod.

5

How can the voices of women be so terrible?

> Hecabe feels the walls of this city
> crumbling inside her, hears the wind
> keening through them. First her children,
> then her children's children, dead.
> She is whirling back towards uncreation
> where only one sound fills the darkness.

They *hate* her screaming.

6

Cassandra kept that death inside her,
did not try to foretell it.
Her desolation is that she can only *know*
the future – never change it,
or glimpse how else it might have been.
A boy runs through olive groves in sunlight.

7

A huge hand is clinging
to the hand of the victor.
He tries to wipe it off –
on walls, stones, trees;
(even his sword cannot unwedge it) –
not realising it is there
to congratulate him.
Its grey, bloodstained fingers
tighten round his –
ingratiating; pledging
loyalty, undying service.

Cassandra

There was nothing original in what she said —
for instance, *All wars end in defeat for all.*
They'd heard it before, and everyone agreed
she was totally wrong. So why did they
lock her away, pay someone to guard her?

They dreamed of smothering her, cutting
her tongue, but somehow couldn't.
She was more beautiful then Helen.
They liked to picture her out there
in that stone cage, surviving, dying.

Apollo had spat in her mouth
when she refused him, put a curse
on his gift — that should have taught her
to have kept that tongue locked up.
Now, no-one believed they believed her.

She, who knew her own end would be
rape and murder, told herself this cell
was a haven. *If only, oh if only…*
A doorway of light shone at the centre
of the floor; dry leaves shuffled, whispered.

Helen

For every spotlit myth, a million shadows.
Helen enjoys the privilege

of walking free in any place,
among the unseen women.

Now, after a royal marriage, a headstrong lover,
a war — what will be left?

Each dawn she walks alone to the sea,
steps into flesh-pricking coolness.

Breathing slowly, she wades against the tide
then, at her own moment,

enters that flux, that tension —
her body poised, moving freely,

inside the wave.

Andromeda

She was the first pin-up.
Naked and bejewelled
she was chained to a rock
then thrown by heavy-breathing
winds into wild postures:
at each new angle, lightning
popped like a photographer's flash.

The gold circling her neck
matched her hair, the emeralds
her eyes, the rubies her nipples,
and the amethysts those bruises.

In lulls of wind, she pulled
against iron, stood almost straight.
The sky was a mouth swallowing her,
the sun a glimmering eye.
Lolling in the tide, a sea dragon
slithered and gurgled
like some vast collective slob.

From afar, Perseus saw her first
as a creature writhing on a rock;
close-up, she was a whirlpool
of rage and terror and shame.
The dragon he changed to stone
with hardly a thought.
But his strength almost failed him
in breaking those chains.

Looking away from her nakedness,
he smooths her ankles, wrists.
she waits for the moment
when he will meet her eyes.

The Pool

He has given her this room of mirrors, in which she is bored;
she may speak to him only when he speaks to her.

He spends most of his time by the pool. What is it he sees,
staring down at its tiled floor – some classical coin

with shimmering bronze face? He is as beautiful as a dolphin
but never swims. She often does. She likes the splashing cry

of the water as her long arms slice through vivid green.
Why does he never look at her? He is always looking down –

even into his glass as they sit in the evening by the pool.
'Have you had a nice day?' (he stirs and pokes his ice);

'... *a nice day?*' she echoes, desolate.
                                        Oh, but she loves him!
Once she swam the pool's whole length to surprise him,

curving up to where he gazed soulfully, teardrops pocking
the chlorine. At first he did not see her face,

then – when she was out of breath, but still smiling –
those clear eyes glazed with shock and he looked away.

She did not hear the slapping of her feet on concrete
as she walked inside, then dripped up the long, soft stairs

to her room. 'With only mirrors to keep me company
I shall waste away, waste away,' she thought

but could not say – as usual, the words stuck in her throat.
And she curled into herself, hiding from all those faces.

Stretched out flat by the pool, he too loved and wasted,
had not even sensed her walking away, her stifled sigh.

Leda's Story

'I thought you were one of my kind,' he said;
then, crestfallen: 'I thought you'd be thrilled.'

To be fair, it was late, and I was a strange one
for squatting out among rushes, waiting

to hear and feel the new tide slapping in
with cool, subtle shadings of wind.

It was such a hot night… My white skin
must have flashed under the moon;

perhaps he saw the wings that —
against all opinion to the contrary —

I know lie just beneath my shoulder blades
and, at moments approaching happiness,

edge and widen into air.
I had no need of those wings thrashing above me.

Now a voice from the swan enjoins me
to turn into a myth

this sordid disturbance of a dream.
'Total belief is all I ask,' he says,

'— or, failing that, the skill to act its presence.'
Gods always ask for your everything, twice.

If I nestle deep down inside the mud, a new self
may hatch and arise, as if from fire…

Or will it be some old self, unreconciled
to these nights of yearning, disquiet:

waiting for an answer that will not raise up
the ghost of some more painful question?

Danaë

Pennies from heaven —
a celestial dew!

Artists show your garments
conveniently askew...

With immaculate conceptions
there's so little to do —

you just lie there pretending
you're looking at the view.

Not being raped but being rained on,
it's difficult to sue.

Should you sleep with an umbrella
in case he tries to renew

your acquaintance with a brief
shower or two?

Weaver

So many stories to be woven.
      She worked with a furious patience,
            conjuring through dream-weary eyes
                  the starred brightness of spiderwebs.
Within, an answering light brought
      warmth to her designs, her fingers
            summoned forest, seascape, town,
                  in facetted jewel-shapes.
Giving her utmost, she thought herself
      without rival – and was,
            surpassing Athena's artistry.
                  Stung, the goddess decreed
a duel – in tapestry.
      Her subject was the gods,
            vast in their pomp, their vengeful pride –
                red splashing the purple.
Arachne, at the far end of the room,
      wove rape after rape
            by gods of mortals:
                  Leda, Europa, Danaë…
'A groundling's view!' – so Athena judged
      and punished Arachne
            for her skill, her truth.
                  (Ah, the smallness of gods.)
Now, ringed planet, nucleus of atom,
      she waits in a network of dew
            to catch and hold the sky,
                  moves with every wind,
anchored close to earth…
      Trapped in that tiny globe,
            her self is inexhaustible:
                  it spins and spins.

Demeter

Once I wished something splendid for her;
now I think, *Let her be joined to*
any man with his nose above ground.

Each year she returns from that airless
dark as from a devouring dream
whose memory is never quite dispersed
until it must be lived again.

Sometimes, a kind of death comes to
immortals, we lose our power,
are whirled into a chaos
for which earth and sunlight are no cure.

She saves me from this, surrenders me to it:
my daughter, who brings the flowers back;
who will be childless.

Underworld

Eurydice stayed, abandoned by a glance.
Persephone stays and leaves, moves between
harrowing and rebirth continually.
Her home is the journey between the two,
her place of rest the moment before
she steps into life or death again.
What was at first confusion, grief,
has become a dance of fulfilment
and loss, stasis and flowering.
If there could be some final resurrection
she would long for it as a haven
yet distrust it – *this* is what she knows.
She gathers herself: exhausted beyond belief,
renewing herself through the centuries.

Orpheus in the Underworld

Invisible but there in the eerie dimness:
all manner of creatures from the daylit world,
an animal breathing beneath lyre and voice.
Slowly becoming present: tree, blade of grass,
closed wings compressing gold, obsidian.
Pollen moves through warming air, bees
from perfumed flower to flower.

                            (*What hour of day,*
what season? murmurs Persephone, in dream.)

Eurydice's feet touch grass, pass by
the sleeping snake. However high or deep,
each note she hears is at the centre,
draws her towards it. She pauses,
(*So many turnings, returnings…*), at the edge
of a meadow she can almost see.

Arion

The crew of the vessel bearing him on his return journey… determined to kill
him for his wealth… They did, however, grant the bard's request that he be
allowed to sing once more before dying. Arion put on his full minstrel's regalia
and began to sing a hymn to Apollo. Seeing that many dolphins, attracted by his
song, were playing about the ship, he leaped into the sea. One of the dolphins
took him on its back and carried him to the shore at Taenarum.

His chanted words were a sea they swam in —
dolphins wreathing the ship where Arion sang
to save his life. He sang without fear,
with ancient formality, dressed in
the dignity of his minstrel's robes.
That set him free to move through sounds like a dolphin,
to be at one with a sea of echoing pathways:
his song was a bright strand woven amongst them.

Then he leapt into water, his dolphin-voyage
a speeding through chill and sunlight —
each fragment of spray a drop of gold-
within-crystal. His homeland began where
that great line of energy broke on sand.
He walked through it, hearing a wordless singing.

Daedalus

Minos... promised to reward anyone who could pass a linen thread through [a Triton shell]... Fastening a gossamer thread to an ant, [Daedalus] bored a hole at the point of the shell and lured the ant up the spirals by smearing honey on the edges of the hole. Then he tied the linen thread to the end of the gossamer and drew that through as well.

Mythic artefacts, the wrought gold
of centuries, gathered to my name.
I had but one pair of eyes through which
the jewelled light shone, one pair of hands
to serve the intricacy of vision.
Between the dual voids of uncreation,
extinction, one shapes a frail offering —
much as this ant, weaving its gossamer
path inside the spiral shell of art.

My labyrinth, gold honeycomb, survive
only in story: like the child I made
they've melted into air, dissolved into
the sea — under that eye which transfigures,
whose gaze we can never return.

Icarus

The sea's turquoise skin, unbroken by white;
mountain-spined islands; minute cities
huddled on hill tops.
                    Sometimes clouds veil
my sight, in a trance I imagine
gliding over the world's edge, looking down,
or plummeting into the Underworld
through a volcano core.
                    What I long for
is to hover like a falcon in the wind:
how furiously, delicately, it works
to be still, the point which sees all else.
I struggle against the unwieldiness
of wings, climb into purer and purer air,
my body dissolves, my spirit floats –
a golden shroud drawn into the heart of light.

Glaucus, Son of Minos

His young son is lost –
Minos orders the seer to find him.

The cellar flickers round his candle:
Polyeidus contemplates, as they close,

an owl's eyes, ochre and tawny,
points to the jar brimming with honey.

A serpent swirls, re-enters the jar,
as the body is raised aloft

into a circle of lamps, faces...
'Give him life,' intones the king –

then, as he breathes, 'Teach him
your secrets: stay here till he learns.'

When, at last, the seer may leave,
he has Glaucus spit in his mouth,

frees him from so much wisdom.
An image of coiling light

is all the boy retains – light,
gold and sinewy, connecting him

to that sweet, curved darkness.

Midas

Not just golden hair, golden wheatfields and golden wine.
          Now, all of solid gold: his caged nightingale,
          the beehive, mayflies on lotus leaves...
          everything becoming bankable –
          even the cockroach cached inside a royal glove,
                              spy into scarab.

Gold-fleshed women flashed their million-dollar smiles –
          so much brightness! He wore sunglasses
          which turned opaque, glittered heavily.
          At night, his body clamped to chill lumps,
          he sensed the walls, the very air, somehow
                              shining through blackness.

And each morning, bread as inedible as stone...
          Inside the stream's dark absolution
          he rests – then steps into an ordinary day
          with the sun's radiance reaching toward him
          from so far: tentative, soft –

                              a beggar's touch.

Sisyphus in Prison

No tension, nothing to press against.
Only the body's strength defeating itself;
the grey smell that inhabits breath, clothes;
a leaden weight in loins and belly.

Towers of stone; coloured television
showing the world out there,
big as my toenail... So what do I see?
    Politics as grand larceny.

        Secret plans for mass slaughter
        handled like religious texts.
        Poisons leak into the unborn,
        claiming an eye, a heart.

They tell us we are the poison,
and must be locked up here –
would bury us alive, were we not
so lost inside their unconscious.

In the middle of the night, pain
raw and insistent as a kidney stone
keeps me awake. Time
lays over me its smothering blanket.

Nemesis is a sour sexual fantasy
played over and over,
her body nebulous, her smile
vacuous, framing sharp teeth.

Atlas

The chiropractor's fingers dig into tight flesh,
her calm voice probes, 'Couldn't you carry less?'
'If I let go for a moment, the sky will fall in.'

'Can't you see any way out?' With gritted teeth:
'I've got to concentrate, hold everything together!'
'Same time next week?' She opens her appointment book.

It contains the names of many people called Atlas.
'Wish I could shift my cares to you for a while!' I say,
putting on the charm. The bill slides towards me:

'Ninety dollars – I'll unburden you of that much.'
All told, a costly venture, in a life without reward:
I only know I'm alive because my shoulders hurt!

Most likely, my fate is to become a kind of mountain,
vastly insensible, with a permanent list – you see them
in boardrooms: old mountains with glinting pince-nez,

fixed agendas, and huge heaps of metal in the bank.
Oh, the more I petrify, the more I disintegrate!
Isn't there someone out there who'll save me?

All I've got here's a woman with bony, questioning fingers:
'Ever tried yoga breathing?' (Yoga breathing? Help!)
World, if I have a breakdown, it'll be your fault!

Teiresias

Drag queen (retired)
back in a suit and sober tie –
almost convincing

but for face flesh sagging
under the memory of
too much make-up;

lashes burdened
at fluttering moments
by blue ghosts of mascara;

mouth a little too wrinkled
even for your wide
slipstream of years.

You re-entered woman
in the only way you could,
mimed her movements

till finally a birth into
this new/old self,
this serviceable enigma.

What to do but be
philosophical, though
it's difficult to rest

inside a body that knows
almost everything
about what it's not.

These days, you give advice
from unpursed lips,
point up plain truths

deviously/directly
— as is *de rigueur*
for prophets.

The envious and the curious
only pretend to believe
while they drink in

as if it were nectar
the atmosphere around you,
scan unseeing eyes

for signs — for swords of light
carving that shining
grey dusk like lasers...

When they go — sometimes,
this fusion, this dissolving,
as shadows slide back

beneath skin,
and all that you have lived,
you become.

From 'The Monsters Talk Back'

Minotaur

Whatever my provenance
I'm an image in your mind,
that ancient maze:

a god hungry for sacrifice,
a conscious animal trapped
in the anguish of flesh.

You will come upon me
like a random memory.
We may clash; try to resolve

what cannot be resolved;
or choose to ignore each other.
Then you may leave. I must stay.

I've so much time to think
here in the silver darkness,
I begin to see the maze entire,

sense you threading towards me,
feel what look your face will wear
when you come upon me

sitting on my throne embedded
in dung, singing softly to myself,
knowing so much, so little.

Dragon and Non-Violent Hero

The non-violent hero is the one
who is waiting for the dragon's
scales to fall off,
though it has lived for a millenium,
will survive another.

The dragon watches the hero
      who has no scales,
      cannot breathe fire, or fly,
      and who *claims* not to
      covet the treasure –
the dragon watches the hero
sleeping in a corner of its cave,
with curiosity, with tenderness...

It stirs the fire, thinking.

Typhon

He was truly the worst of all:
vicious, cunning as a snake
and highly inflammable –
a vast oil slick swirling across oceans.

What if he had succeeded
in toppling the gods
and now ruled the universe,
the voices of a hundred men and animals
issuing from his hundred heads?

Well?

Menagerie

Not all of them were changed to swine.
She kept experimenting,
intuiting their hidden selves,
unlived wishes:
> body of a lion; head of a horse;
> wolverine eyes; voice of nightingale.

Dignity had nothing to do with it:
they stood, composed, liberated,
accepting their own natures.

Then she tried transforming one
into the image of her own desire.
She concentrated: would this work —
the most quixotic magic of all?

> A crinkly whirr... Was that a dragonfly —
> out the window before she could blink,
> skywriting in bronze across a rainbow?

The wrong page, the wrong potion —
why does she always get light-headed
when it's been raining?
> It's dusk:
now she must mix their feed —
for that she will need her wits about her.

The Graeae

Yet another set
of women in triplicate.
They share an eye and a tooth between them –
a capacity the well-run modern state
might wish for many of us.

And what are these women doing?

They are creating
a history of the world.

The facts take them a long time to digest,
and it's a strain writing by a single candle,
with a single eye;

but they have three minds.
each of them razor-sharp,
well used to remembering, anticipating,
the smallest light in any darkness.

Oracle

1
The message is written
on a page of water
above which a crystal drop
trembles.

2
The message is the apple
slightly beyond reach
that falls at its own moment
into the hand no longer
waiting, wanting.

3
The message is the seed
inside the shell's spiral.

4
To interpret the message
requires only one thing:
the invention of new ways
of interpreting.

5
Oracles merely magnify
what is in the nature of things –

fruitfulness, disaster
experienced more keenly

because they come as
an answer to a question.

6

Advice is harmful.

I give it only to those
who'll never act on it —

the very ones who
always ask for it.

7

I speak in metaphor to the literal-minded,
in plain words to the suggestible;
I am a poet and a scientist.

If this creates havoc
I'm not responsible.

I play the trickster only on Thursdays
or when the moon is in its third quarter
or when a tide of sea mist drowns the valley.

8

An oracle must use
every ambiguity,
stop just this side of
despoiling language.

Thus the listener is
forced to dislocate
words, dig under them —
to where networks
of roots wind down to
the inverted tree.

9

My one gift is that I can hear
the earth's heartbeat.

Do you really think I don't
know what you're up to?

10

Imagination is full knowledge of the possible.
I offer half-knowledge of the inevitable.

11

And my own fate?

'What?' 'When?' 'Who?' 'How?'
– not interesting questions.

I never ask them.

12

My eyes are accustomed to the dimness;
it sharpens them.

My owl and I
gaze at each other across this space.

Only when too much light enters
does she sleep,

sweeping through
thickets of dream, murmuring.

13

Prophecy is the fabled
honeycomb of gold
wrought by Daedalus.

Cold as eternity
it is composed of spaces
waiting to be filled

with wisdom – a honey
that holds warmth, light,
carries the scent of flowers.

14

Though earth is my element
I can hear the sea beyond the mountains.

It gives us word and chaos;
shape, and dissolution –

rhythms reversing
then flowing over us,

as our ears echo
with wavefall, wingbeat,

and the almost audible
song of the dolphin

threading in half-moon arcs
through crystal darkness.

Erysichthon

In Demeter's sacred grove
the Dryad within the oak
cried out as he chopped,
the wood bled.

Nemesis decrees
his hunger will intensify
the more he eats.

He plunders to meet his need
till there is no more left
to plunder

and it is his own flesh
he gnaws – hearing,
as if from another body,
cries that he cannot heed.

Heracles' Lunch

Disliking the drink set before him, he struck Cyathus, the cupbearer,
with one finger only, but killed him none the less.

A cupbearer killed
for a disappointing sip.

The host's three sons slain
for serving the wrong
portion of the beast.

Lucky that only Heracles
behaves like a hero
at the table.

Four dead before
the meal is underway.

What's for dessert,
and who will serve it?

Ares

He has no memory,
and what he sees is that nothing is happening…

only life itself — pigeons on terraces,
hot dinners, urchins in a field.

He wants something, anything, to happen
that will change all this.

Walking, later, through the ruined village,
he says over and over, *This is real.*

But he doesn't believe that, either.
They are lying there, they are dead.

He just doesn't believe it.
He still wants something to happen.

Flute Music

The ancient Sybarites taught some of their horses to dance to flute music.
This sometimes led to embarrassment on the battlefield.

More than the bracelet of massed shields
it was the light on the flanks of prancing horses
that mesmerised the enemy...

In pricked ears, the dulcet breath
of wind through high trees
as a blushing warrior broke rank, sashayed

on his light-footed beast towards them –
rupturing their line, their faces frozen
while they waited with clutched spears,

above earthbound hooves,
watching man and horse frisk, whirl,
go through their paces –

disarmed by that errant sight
as if by a centaur waltzing.

Nike

At exactly which point
after the battle
does the Angel of Death
meet the Angel of Victory?
What do they say to each other?
How do they look at each other?

As his tent is being packed up
on a distant hill —
cognac, concubine, playing cards, maps —
a general smokes a cigar,
hazing the morning light around him
as it grows sharper, brighter.
Too sophisticated a man to indulge,
even for one moment, in triumphalism,
he is brooding again.
He is always brooding.
Nevertheless, he believes he sees
over the slaughterfield
a kind of aura, a sheen,
a flickering, a fluttering, a something...
It could be wings.
It could be a woman with wings —
almost invisible, catching
for a split second, the ambivalent light.
He waves the smoke away.
The scene is now clear-cut.
He coughs, calls for his horse,
drains his coffee.

the sixth swan

Rapunzel

At dawn, her stone-framed face;
hair spread out in the room's darkness.

Gold shrouds the misted pines,
scrolls over the lake, finds her.

All day, bronze enters her hair;
her cheeks grow amaryllis apples.

The forest's shadow is a meniscus
round that great brimming tear.

As she steps back, the noon's glare
slides down her, brow to belly.

Rapunzel stands, weaving her strength
into a braid, thinking:

Whatever has happened, or will happen,
the lake is there; and the tower

dwells in me, and I within it:
a key hidden inside a lock.

She watches the wind's fingers
trail a nap on silver velvet;

unsettle then recompose
the snow-blue spruces.

The Twelve Dancing Princesses

In later life, none could recapture
    that long season of dancing nights –
      the enchanted risk of them:
        at twelve, the flight down steps;
          silk dresses rustling through groves
            of gold, diamond, and silver
          to the boat trip on moon-filmed water,
        the lake sighing and whispering its secrets
      as their perfect princes rowed them
    towards the underground castle
then danced the soles out of their shoes
    and plied them with wine
      and were impeccable
        as they rowed them home
          silent with ecstasy
            over the pear-shaped lake –
          princesses with dancing eyes
        returning to their locked room.
      Only the soldier who'd shadowed them,
    who'd stepped on the hem of the youngest
(her half-lit face half-turned)
    brought back mementos –
      three precious twigs
        and the goblet he'd sipped from
          while partnering each princess,
            invisibly, in his magic cloak.
        Then the exposé, the opulent evidence.
      The eldest was forced to marry him,
    the others became royal wives
  in far kingdoms where they had
balls and ballgowns to order.
    They glittered with riches
      and smiled convincingly –
        but never again would they
          dance their slippers through.

Strange jewellery they had made —
gold leaves veined with diamonds,
and tiny silver twigs
that they wore like open secrets.
Often, too, they remembered
the lantern that sung across the lake
as if a star were caged in it.
In the cellar of the first castle
were heaped all the dancing shoes
full of centipedes and mice
and ropes of dust, and mouldering
wine from a leaky cask.
Beside them were old letters,
sere as parchment, and a book
with a rusty lock, containing
stories that sometimes ended:
'And the mouth of the last person
who told this story is still warm.'

The Frog Prince

She looked down into secret water.
Beneath archipelagos of lilies:
males, clamped on doormat backs;

a frenzied globe of them
vying for the female at their centre.
March became April —

wide-legged, they wrinkled
into exhaustion, afloat on
islands of sunlit spawn.

One day, an errant throw
left her golden ball stranded on dankness.
A stone spoke from the grass

with squat authority,
his words swimmingly fluent
but for those belches of marsh gas:

he offered help... A concertina-dive
through rotting weeds nudged the ball
back to her feet on frilled ripples.

His gaze swivelled: he ventured to hope
he might (*burble gulch*) call on her?
Noblesse oblige... A banquet, then.

An endless white damask cloth;
lit towers brimming with tallow.
Inside her goblet's shadow, he was slime.

Her tongue slid over silver
inlaid with ivory — no comfort there:
his bottom-of-the-pond eyes drank her in.

A bilious attack, first;
the vapours; then, hysterics —
she'd let him have it!

After, she lay in her locked room,
her deepest tears unable to be shed;
a seething emptiness.

That chance look found him poised
on her slipper: obsidian eyes
shone from fine gold rims.

Her breathing stalled, her heart contracted,
she felt murderously afraid — so flung him,
a warty arrow, into the chandelier!

Frozen forms lay shattered, melting,
as she stood among tears of crystal, and wept light.
There were no strong arms to hold her,

though from somewhere, a princely voice,
pellucid as spring water.
                    She leant closer,
heard his desperate words: 'Kiss me!'

The Sixth Swan

The six shirts were finished, except for one that still lacked its left sleeve… The moment the shirts touched them, their swan skins fell off, and there stood her brothers, strong and handsome. Only the youngest lacked his left arm and had a swan's wing in place of it.
     – 'The Six Swans'

A waterfall of feathers spills from his left shoulder.
He's tempted to tilt his body sideways, limp,
convulse his features, but finds with practice
a measured stride, an expression – half-open,
half-closed – that will meet the situation.

Wealthy enough to hire a tailor of genius,
leisured enough to choose a life of letters,
he slides a brocaded cuff across vellum,
trailing *feuilletons*, odd gnomic poems:
monocles to quiz moonlight, seed unearthly fires.

Above sloped fingers, his quill embroiders air –
stops – moves resolutely on…
                              He has picked up
the dropped stitch of his first, lost life.
There will be lapses, eccentricities, of course.
For one, he frequents the highest tower to see

flocks pinwheel the sunset, fracture in storm
or swim through cloud-surf, breasting noon's topaz.
At such times his eyes become dangerous jewels
that fade to dullness when someone is sent
to guard him: 'My, but that spectacle is ravishing –'

(a sidelong glance), 'they reach such heights!'
'Yes,' he rejoins wearily, 'it *is* a long way down.'
But he's not tempted. If he feels a tremor
of that winged life pass through him,
his whole body unnerved, displaced from itself,

as a great white shadow twitches and tingles –
athirst to be silvered by sunlight, to arrow through
cobalt space above miles of conifers –
well, that is all so much rhetoric...

                                 His wing
settles into his side like moulded parchment.

It is only having two arms again would break him.
And had he two wings it would sadden – he'd be
a homunculus-bird, a lard-wrapped angel...
He climbs the steps of the tower. It's midnight.
The sky is a page of stars he can't write on,
a compendium of invincible memories.

Bearskin

The devil wears a green coat
and drives a hard bargain.
We met and made our pact
in a circle of trees on a heath.

For the next seven years I stayed
unwashed, my hair grew thick as felt,
clotted with grease and dust;
my hands became claws;

I said not one word of prayer.
The deep pocket of the green coat
bred ducats like fleas;
and my cloak and my bed

was the skin of the bear
I'd killed to prove my courage:
a second skin, a second self —
morning and night; year in, year out.

At first, I lived high off the hog —
who wouldn't? — travelled abroad
in plush coaches, not minded
to let stricken faces stop me.

I was a wealthy beast,
and had the devil's own strength.
But came the day no mirror
could decipher me;

grass poked from my collar;
my bear-cloak made children
and small animals
run from me in terror.

Yet through those seven years
I bought the prayers of the poor,
my heart stayed a warm hearth.
There was an old man I found

huddled in tears at an inn.
My gold saved him from despair.
In gratitude, his daughter
offered to be my bride.

I broke my ring, gave her half —
then vanished until the moment came
when I could stand in that
circle of wind-bent trees

ready to return the green coat
and force the devil to scrub
each grain of dirt from me,
and to scissor my nails and hair —

restoring me to my self.
That done, the half-rings were joined,
my bride's hand could rest in mine
and a joyous peace reign.

Thus I learnt ways of life
other than war, my body's courage
took root in my soul — and never again
would the devil touch me.

The Robber Bridegroom

The bird caged inside my head sang:
How we don't know what we know!
How we know what we don't know!
        as I followed the trail that led
        to the forest's dead heart.

There I came upon a house,
made of shifting walls and shadows,
encircled by bare trees full of ravens.
        If this is a dream, it's one that could
        kill you! sang the bird

as I crossed the threshold to drift through
airless rooms, echoing with ghost-voices,
where silvery rats eyed me —
        sentinels standing their ground.
        Hide! Flee! Save yourself! Save me!

cried the voice of an old woman
as my bridegroom came in, flanked by
men bearing a maiden they forced
        to drink yellow wine, green,
        then black wine, until her heart burst.

So they became festive as they
sliced her on the table,
her ringed finger flying into my lap
        near my own ring finger, as I crouched
        behind ripped, bloody curtains.

As if everything I saw there
I had already seen, my face
stayed calm and unchanged.
        At midnight, I stepped over
        the dead-drunk bodies, and walked home.

Our wedding day. I welcomed
my bridegroom, and when the time came
to give the toast, raised my glass high,
and spoke of a house, deep in the forest,
where a maiden, unvoiced by fear –

(*'But my darling, it was a dream…'*) –
drained glass after glass, her lips turning
yellow, then green, then black.
And I told how scarlet wine
spilled from her limbs as the robbers

chopped and were festive, severing
the ring finger from her white hand.
'*But my darling… only a dream.*'
Now all my guests were smiling,
each pointing their ring finger at him.

I held my own hand out, and pointed
her finger straight at him
while smiling into his eyes:
'*Darling, it was just a dream.*'
Now he shrank within himself

as if trying to unmake himself –
only *his* heart did not burst.
Then he came out of his dream
and remembered the day, long since,
he chose to be ruled by it.

The wine on the table was the crimson
of blood and pain. I drank deeply
then broke my glass, ready to choose
peace, have done with all this –
to follow rumours of joy.

Jorinda and Joringel

Forest Walk

Once inside the forest we went deep
        then deeper, on tranced footsteps till –
               by what twilight mood entrammelled? –
we became locked in melancholy
and stood beneath frozen pines
        as if time had forsaken us.
               Forcing herself to sing
        Jorinda freed us – we ran wildly on
till we came to thick walls
        alive with tentacles of creeper.
               Her song transformed, mid-flight,
        into bird sound, her body
a fluttering shape, first swiped at
        then shrouded by batwing folds.

Witch

In her castle of cages
the continual trilling
of songbirds.

No need to prick eyes –
they sing so piercingly
of what they lack:

draw on memory,
inner oracle, as they lift
into vibrato flight.

Each maiden sees
her image multiplied
a thousand times...

Dirty claws sprinkle
song-seeds, place pearls
in bowls of water.

At midnight, bats whizz
from tower and turret —
inside-out birds

encoding space with glass notes:
a pitchless descant above
the music that never stops.

Jorinda's Song

Nightingale calls to robin,
who calls to lark...

Our voices throb
in this airless dusk.

Sunlight slants in:
wicker bars stripe us.

We sing our inexhaustible
hymn, open wings

to distant warmth.

Bats

They fly from her dusty black clothes,
halo that plague of warts, her face.

She runs to watch them cancel stars,
sign the moon's radioactive paper

then dive earthwards for blood: tube-tongues
slide in above hoof, at neck vein.

Back home they'll cling, gothic bunions,
to vaults draped with varicose webs.

Favourites sleep clamped to her cloak
or cradle her breasts, snug as infants.

Joringel

I woke in some other place.
My quest to find her led me
up avalanches of time,
through treadmill circuits.

In defeat, I dreamed of
an amaryllis, its one dewdrop
a diamond eye guiding me
back to the castle — where

gate after gate sprang open,
the portal of every cage.
The maidens' wings fell away.
They re-entered their bodies,

singing with reborn voices
as they streamed into the day.
All but one... Her hand on a sill,
Jorinda turned to me,

her eyes undimmed by
eclipse, sunlight wreathing
her unbound hair.

Jorinda

Beyond the forest, a field
of buttercups silvered by rain.

I stayed wordless, resting my throat.
When the lark ascended

to sing inside the day moon,
my gaze traced her dizzying path

and hovered — as did my lifted hand,
(the other on Joringel's arm).

Tides of cold light, of the fragile green
beneath our feet, ebbed away

then flowed back, as the lark —
pivot of starred hill and pearl sky —

dropped to her woven nest,
its flurry of diamond beaks.

In the Castle

My sorrowing eyes fill with
row upon row of empty cages.

In this castle of echoes
I'll find some long-locked room

to breathe dead space in —
and so die, by surviving.

*

No! – away with all that!
I'd like to fly up near the moon,
have it silhouette my head
then turn left and surprise it –
dive into a crater of hot lead
and have a bath! Sing my lungs out!

*

Here in this chamber
my bats are fruit ripening
on splintery beams;
shopping bags on chandeliers.

I pluck them at will
and hold their pug faces
to my breast, singing my song
that no one can hear.

*

Today, I'll make the sun
go down early, lay a fire.

Tinderbox and kettle;
burnt toast; tin whistle.
And brandy – lots!

I will leave my toes unwashed
till they grow a thistle.

Rumpelstiltskin

Brought undone by mindless glee,
by announcing himself to the universe
just a little too loudly.

Name-riddle-self –
he goes on singing,
in the cellar, in the tower –
too mad to be lonely,
captive of a broken spell.

A survivor of deadlocked nights,
she has become a singer herself,
spins gold back into straw
to feed the creatures who companion her.

Her hair's bright gold has turned to white;
no one else is there.
This is not a fairy story.

She steps through the doorway
to stroke sinews of couch grass,
feel winter air.

Wrapped in a silver net
the cradle rocks
under the linden tree
under the white sun.

From 'Ashputtle'

Time

The white bird blessed my tears
but when the turning point came,
gowned me in midnight sunlight,
had me driven to the ball.

The white bird told me to live,
remembering – but, when hope
knelt before me, to cast off
the ash-stained clogs,

and let my right foot slip into
the glass shoe that would change
the shape of my life.
                        Present joy,
all splendours to come,

have been paid for in advance
by years of sorrow,
by time that lay like a pool
of dirty water on my heart.

I know that I must relearn,
again, and always, the moment
of freedom.
                My feet climb
scarred ravines, traverse

summer and winter fields,
pass water meadows
shadowed by homing swallows.
I make maps; I burn them.

The Handless Maiden

The right hand lay stretched out
on her lap: five white suns
about to set, or rising;
brown rainspots sprinkled on earth-flesh.

The left hand opened, cradling itself:
a bowl of sheened pink offered
mainland with promontories,
a chaos of rivulets.

There were grooves, eyelash-fine,
as if hatched by nib or quill;
others, etched with deeper intent –
runes, not-to-be-translated.

Behind knuckles, needlework threads,
cobalt-purple as the tracery on thumbs.
At the wrist, lightning-strike of
lavender, and almost-aquamarine.

The hands met, began to reshape
each other, learn each other, dance...

       What to do but go on imagining
       those hands until they grew back,
       and she could grasp onto life,
       and not let go before life failed her –

       when, cupped by the fingers' cage,
       the poem she has lived
       will sing to soothe her, allay her worst fears,
       deliver her into a painless light sleep.

The Juniper Tree

There is a place beneath the world's tree
where the deepest griefs and wrongs go –
kept alive by those who will not forget:

so that, in time, a bird hatches from
the roots and rises to sing the tale
of what happened – to sing until

the wrong is set right, the death's undone,
and all who suffered receive balm.
(*But this is only a story.*)

So the murdered boy returned home
to live out his childhood
with a charmed vulnerability.

After, his chances matched the rest –
save that, having passed beyond death
he met with life more freely than most,

and, being so steeped in suffering,
found present pain could often
be healed by memory...

Knowing so well the end of all stories,
did he become one of the tellers? –
a tranced presence beside hearths,

nourisher of firelit faces – unfolding
the path through ordeal with confidence,
with a serene air speaking of death,

and revealing, at last, the seed of hope
as if holding up an amber bead
to catch the burning light, then passing it –

with the body of a small moth inside –
passing it unharmed through
the candle's liquid-gold tongue?

The Gold Key

One winter's day, when the ground lay deep in snow, a poor boy
was sent to the forest with a sled to bring back wood...

So perilously cold was he
and so far from home, he must use
some of the wood he'd gathered
to make a fire — or not return at all.

As he dug through snow to clear a space
he found a gold key — and deeper still,
a keyhole set in earth.
His fingers being near frozen,

he made his whole aching body
circle the lock. Then he was in a cavern
lit by small fires, and gradually —
which is the best way — he grew warm.

Above were stalactites full of
pictures and stories, all slowly melting...
Was the boy dreaming this
as he lay merging with snow, or was he

far beneath earth in a haven
where ice and fire meet? Did he in fact
light a snow-fire and crouch by it,
with entranced eyes gazing up

at white needles shrouding fir trees —
imagining the heat he felt
touch each of them, so that those great
pagodas ran with silver light?

Did he make it home with the wood —
to sit by the hearth with his people,
and drink soup till his toes curled,
watching snow whirl like feathers

shaken from a quilt? And was there
a gold key printed on his palm
as he sat listening to the stories
while mutely remembering?

Or did he decide to tell about
the cave of stories shining through ice? —
millennia of stories melting,
and he catching the drops on his tongue?

The Prince (and the Princess)

Just as the prince was setting off to fetch his bride, his mother kissed him, and he forgot everything that had happened and everything he'd meant to do.
— *'The Prince and the Princess'*

The thing is,
you get so very tired:
    the impossible tasks
    the gut-twisting tension
    and there's always three of everything —
you can never rest.

It's the women who have the magic.

First, my beloved
    who tied a knot in her handkerchief,
    struck the earth three times,
    said, 'Earwigs, come!' —
        so that the forest was chopped
        the great pond emptied
        the castle built —
    all in a matter of hours
    by an army of elves.
(I managed to have a nap.)

Next, her mother
    who could not abide me
    and called on supernatural aid
    to block our escape;

    then my own mother
    who caused me to forget my beloved
    as soon as she kissed me:
    the whole slate wiped clean.

This was, of course, terrible,
yet a welcome respite
in that, at last, I got some sleep.

At the crucial moment,
I made up for my lapse by
waking up and waking up and waking up –
oh yes, it never ends...

And even now, though I'm content –
            delivered forever from
            the amnesia of unhappiness –
I still need a wealth of sleep.

In the evenings, my queen is
a poem by candlelight;
but when she ends her enchanted stories with:
            So they divided the Apple of Life
            and ate it together,
            and lived in undisturbed happiness
            to a great age...
I'm always well away.
Servants have to carry me to my chamber.

There is so much to recover from.
The happy ending allows you to rest.

The White Snake

The prince lifted the silver lid, and there it lay –
a long white tongue, self-renewing as he ate of it:
his own tongue mingling with its flesh,
learning to taste the lost language of creatures.

Now he heard, and saw, a new world through them:
arcane owl and nerveless fox; geese,
brassily honking; the dog, warm-eyed and lonely.

Setting forth, he met a fish that, gasping, still spoke –
put it back in the river; obeyed a tiny black voice
and rode around an ant-kingdom;
then slew his horse to feed three starving ravens.

Footsure, footsore, he trudged on – with each mile,
becoming more his own person.
Now he chanced upon her: the difficult princess,
the father's daughter who held all men to ransom:
those impossible tasks; death the price of failure.

He won her hand when the fish he'd saved
brought the lost ring from the depths;
his ant-friends filled twenty sacks with the scattered millet;
and the ravens plucked from the mythic Tree, a golden apple.

The princess ate of its flesh, with each bite gazing further
into his eyes until she could not come out again.
They married; were crowned king and queen.
Heirs were born – and the tale could begin over.

Alone at the table, the youngest princess
finds a salver engraved with snake-like swirls.
She lifts its lid, cuts a thin white slice, and eats.

secret lives

In Conversation

We sat in the room where so often we have talked.
'Listen,' you said, your hand gesturing toward
the window, last daylight fading from your lips.

You got up to open the window, stood against it,
your burgundy dress a cross-shape as you reached
to widen the velvet curtains. I saw the lampshade's

clay-and-honey glow, the orange flare of the fire
and, as you moved back to your chair, the distant
lit room amidst a darkened cluster of roofs.

Now we could hear the blackbirds more clearly:
the two of them half-speaking, half-singing,
through twilight, answering each flute-like call.

In between, the cadenced silences
till fresh notes rose to embellish air,
stream through coolness.

We sat on, hearing the clock,
our own heartbeats, and the soft swinging
of the paper lamp; breezes hinting at summer.

The Power of Mirrors

— their famed, useless objectivity —
may outstare generations before
judgement clouds, a drab silt

blurs peripheral vision:
time's fingernails squeezing in
under bevelled edges.

Contrary to rumour, mirrors
never talk back, remain mute
on matters of fear, vanity, envy.

Neither can they do damage —
unless subject themselves to
a quicksilver wound

that will scar cheeks, gash necks;
a cicatrix-brooch
hovering above an iris.

We are surprised by mirrors only once.
Youth's forthright, uncertain glance
yields to chameleon fascination;

later, a glad-to-be-disappointed gaze
may take hold, or the face resolve
into unreadability.

Mirrors, likewise, cultivate sang-froid.
Even when self-despising eyes
look daggers, infinite slivers

stay intact: one sees them lying
jaggedly dovetailed
beneath smooth phosphorescence...

Midnight, a door is shut,
a room left to its own devices.
A moonstone lake absorbs

the last light-trace, becomes
a photograph of nothing
developing in a bath of darkness.

At dawn, gunmetal grey flares with
ghost-flowers, molten coral.
Then the day's patient work:

an omniscient servant creating
a folio of glimpses,
rubbing the slate-and-stardust oval

clean after each incursion
so that the room dwells within
scrolled gilt again, simply,

its window an inner lens:
framed by fuchsia plush,
an airy veil filters motes that will

dance like atoms in a spotlight;
the drama of ice and fire;
bird shadows' deft mimicry of hands.

Rooms

Could one surprise a room,
fling open a door to discover
some unknown mood of silence

or, in the air, a busyness
one could not quite read —
memories, stored in brick flesh,

now seeping back into space
to be sparked by sunlight
into a sky of milling planets?

Cells, shed from tired skin,
settle in lesions, joins,
enter wood's susceptibility,

so that body and mind, both,
leave their trace, in a chemistry
that brings tremulous pain,

the brute years, to a stillness.
Even when we breathe elsewhere,
the work is being done,

our elements sift into
solidity; are resurrected
as masonry shifts and dust-clouds rise,

so that you cannot see for looking:
the atmosphere of a room
re-entering your skin, your blood —

life recognising itself amidst
dissolution; as foundations stir;
when diamond-blades of light

pierce through and through
what one thought void,
done with.

In the House

Fingers stumble against plates;
a duster flicks ornaments
from their humdrum lives
to splinter on ash-stained hearth;
pot plants noticed too often, die.

Her hand clamps an island
of steak near where she hacks it
as if the flesh of an enemy
newly killed, beyond thought already.

In the end, forks in the drawer
attack her, egg stains return
to scrubbed pans, a whirring
bowl seams a spiral of blood
into creamy blandness.

This is the nemesis sent to one
who does nothing with ease –
the reward for services
rendered in love's absence.

Though it clamours still
for food, the body cries, *All this
is so beside the point!* –

but how can she hear it,
bent to the vacuum's whine
exacting its pound of dust
from shagpile. Then that silence

ringing in her ears
as creeper curls over sills, and
she imagines the whole house
in the garden's forced embrace.

Her gaze shifts to smudges that censor
her face – superimposed on
glass figures by a lake;
a moonlit sea-storm; sunflowers

bursting from the frame
of their petals, from molten centres,
each tip a wanton flame
draining the air she breathes.

Wind

Drag on shoulders and back as you heave
a huge muscle coming apart in your grip,
spilling away from you — rush it out
among leaves in flux, colliding whispers.

One hoist clumps it over the tightrope:
a humped shape flapping absurdist wings.
Next, the pull into smoothness as tears
roll down arm veins, fuse skin and wool.

Damp gathers in vortex of navel,
the belly moulded, with breasts and limbs,
by this erotic shroud. You release it
to a straight fall, remove the template.

Your hair a cubist halo, clothes
darkened by water, you peg the sheet
that knows your impress so well.
Half-sighs, an austere rustling:

this impersonal fabric
has its voices, too. They tell you
to live with your hands on the world,
to uncoil its bundled knots.

Your body itself is a subtle knot
silhouetted by pure air,
its heat transfiguring
cool envelopes you enter:

white planes blankly receiving
sweat, a few trace elements –
till whisked away to be
drowned, then resurrected:

sails for the winds of heaven
to rest against, curved as cheek or hollow
of palm; resisting and surrendering;
teased to life by the merest touch.

Dressmaker

As a girl I loved fabrics, stitching, moulding them to fit.
I remember a flared dress, pink roses on white.
Wearing it with my first high heels, I tottered past
neighbourhood louts slung on a verandah.
From their transistor, Marty Robbins sang,
'A White Sport Coat and a Pink Carnation.'
As I blushed they eyed the smoky summer air.

At sixteen, a slippery silk dress with whorls
of crimson, pinched in with a cummerbund.
With unswerving hips I passed the greengrocer,
an Italian who sighed, whistled, called, in one sound;
his pregnant wife thrusting beans and tomatoes into paper bags.
Her look touched mine: wary, beyond challenge, sisterly.

Ten years of illness next, when I bundled myself
inside coats all summer, wore black as often as not.
Hard to stand straight inside a body so out of kilter.

Since then I have put on the garment of my womanhood.
It marks the curves and leanings of my flesh,
holds in, reveals, what I have come to be,
beyond promise and blight. I know its weight,
its transparency, its rawness, its flawed smoothness.
I wear it now with something close to ease,
with the freedom, almost, of nakedness.

Hourglass in an Interior

On becoming forty

Among unlit candles, vessels of fruit and flowers
on the window seat, I have placed an hourglass.
Its linked bulbs, dusty with sand, mingle
shadows, brass glints, stars from the small spruce;
portray the room in burnished miniature.
I upend the hourglass:

                    a tiny pyramid builds.
With that turning, I constitute a wish –
to ask little of time, seek no reversals –
and accept these gifts:

                    apples, crimson and lime;
candles, milky, blood-red, emerald;
sprigs of honesty arching from moulded clay –
some, pearl-white; others, purple radiating mauve:
the colours of sorrow

                and healing.
The plant holds, resists, light in shapes
akin to the hourglass, angles its sensuous,
papery satin – on which I would like to record
such poems as this.

                By candlelight, the lip-bright berries,
those opal leaves, will make a fine sight.

Accident

It could happen like this.
You turn the corner of another
night, wake foot to the floor
as the car around you
slides down a mountain.

Today, a journey to be made.
You sit stunned in early light
then clutch the keys, persuaded
the dream relives past crashes –
you've had a string of them.

The odds are longer, now,
you think; in fact, they're shorter.

Out from the city, headed for
shifting white distance.
As if you were someone else
you pass through fear, exhaustion,
sudden chokeholds of panic.

Near dusk, it's hunger and loneliness
that propel you, are the fuel
you burn. The car has become
a body aching with miles, a mind
fraught with intentions.

Then the mountains, weaving you
into their folds; the turn
towards glass and chrome
stopped on asphalt.
                  Foot to the floor,
an endless skid on gravel.

Once more, a lesson;
mercifully, no injury to persons,
only brute metal:
the mudguard's turned back
like a skin flap from a wound.

Fine carving... You pray for
eyes that will see levelly.

The Chinese Astronomer

A Chinese astronomer sits opposite me
at a breakfast table in Florence.
He has come from a conference in Trieste.
For two years he has lived in Switzerland.
Something or someone sent him there
and will decide when he goes back
to his wife and his son
who is about to enter Beijing University.
Perhaps he'll return by the end of the year?

I tell him I have been to Padua —
once, Galileo's city —
and climbed its old Observatory tower.
So many stairs, so many stars.

Later that day, he stumbles towards me
in the street, lost and in panic.
'Can you help me?' he pleads,
as if to a stranger,
expecting not to be understood.

That evening, across the table
conversation is difficult,
because he has drunk much,
and I have drunk nothing.
We speak different varieties
of perfect English, mention cities
as if they were bubbles or stars:
Amsterdam. Venice. London. Madrid.

Towards midnight, unlocking my door,
I turn and catch, from the corridor's end,
his fugitive glance
in which despair outstrips all desire,
as if I were the phantom of his wife
destined always to pause at a threshold
then disappear into an unknown room.

At the beginning of the day,
in one of the pauses that was the conversation,
he had said clearly, brokenly,

                    It is too long.

Then his hands had knocked over the sugar bowl:
white glistening mounds on a white tablecloth
that must have seemed as meaningless
as a map of the earth, or of the heavens.

Travelling Alone

There are the creature comforts, of course:
warmth of an iced miniature of gin,
plastic cups filled with dark traces of tea.

Then daydreams... the feeding on
longing, memory.
Only in true sleep can you escape them.

Here you welcome them, leave the door
half-open so they can pass in and out —
old ghosts; wisps of prescience.

Your hand comes to rest on a satchel
of poems, books — isolating, radial.
Time. As usual, passing. When

will you be there? Where? Numbness now.
All the distance you have travelled
swings on to your back as you prepare to leave.

The relief of earth again, every footfall
a mark on a map. The tension of creating
that map, not knowing.

Then you give yourself one moment:
stand calmly, in possession.
Yourself alone.

Night Driving

You concentrate, refusing
siren-fantasies,
sleep's tidal pull; hold
each slippery moment,
and the completed journey,
in one thought.
Salt lakes, marshlands,
the sea-line's whispering crash.
In sudden moonlight
the wind changes hills
from one green to another –
somewhere out there; on all sides.
Tyres on stones; speeding beams
startle eyes drugged by
so much darkness.
You are pulled by a thread
over hundreds of miles,
making your small mark
in the dust, the dew,
going back to where,
using the headlights as a torch,
you will fumble with keys,
re-enter a gathered
stillness – giving thanks,
the house totally lit up
before dawn comes.

Venice Notebook

1

At first you want to restore each facade,
remove each trace of centuries-old dirt,
modern acid − all to please your eye.

Next morning, a river of light bathes
wounds in crimson plaster; a sparrow
perches among ancient geraniums.

You open windows, breathe − you are here.

2

From a balcony, greenery grows down
towards a white sheet edged with heavy lace,
and another, sky-blue with swirls of cloud;
both are of vast proportions.

Behind glass, an interior gleams
with cameos, figurines, spring flowers −
life flourishing in miniature,
with scope enough for grand gestures.

3

The water's glitter
makes its way up walls,
a ghostly creeper,

moving inside your room,
across the ceiling,
down your arms

as you sit, writing.
Once, music floats over
a sill crowded with tulips.

You hear Vivaldi
swallow-weaving
Venetian light,

imagine that light flowing
over him as he sits,
dreaming, inscribing.

4

With people, I only glance, stroll past;
but with cats, pigeons, and masks,
I am studious.

The pigeons see all,
see nothing, mesmerised by
a dream of showers of corn.

Cats give back
stare for stare, too insolent
to take offence.

And the masks are watching
before I stop at their windows,
and as I walk away —
not looking back, unsnubbable.

5

Pigeons live in crevices, behind gargoyles —
they live everywhere.

Today, thronging the square,
they form a collective of bright-eyed indifference.

Suddenly, the air is fanned by wings —
hundreds are following an old man to his door.

Soon he stands among them
flinging seeds from a paper bag.

They are his disciples: layered wing on wing,
they feed on his smallest words.

6

The mask-maker stands in the dusk
at the back of his shop, hunched over
a sun which radiates from his hands;
its gilded rays frame a too-cheerful grin.
On the bench, a new moon smiles softly.

At Carnival you become what you are not,
or what you are — some secret self.
But who will assume this old woman's face
with its maze of wrinkles
and Medusa-tangle of white hair?

Centering the display, it is surrounded by
Scorpion, Double Face, Jolly Old Man.

7

From her verandah, my neighbour
starts arguments with passers-by,
lifts agèd hands in greeting.

Above the canal's grey sheen,
light etches her face more deeply
each year. No need to tell her

that life's river is always moving on.
Witch-like, she contemplates
mist, falling away or rising,

geraniums blazing;
hears cat fights, the play
of children, songbirds in cages.

8

On the cobblestones by the canal
young girls are playing late,
will come to no harm.

Their laughter punctuates words
I am beginning, at last,
to recognise:
                domani, luna, stupido.

When Carla's mother calls
down to her, the sound is
a shimmering orange scarf
unfurled in the night air,
hovering.

9

As the island becomes
a half-familiar labyrinth

you uproot yourself,
probe *vicolo*, cul-de-sac,

till you light on a hotel
known six years before

in another existence
you do not want to remember.

Clean, anonymous, austere,
it is eminently erasable.

You turn tail, head for the water.

10

As if it were a bar, young men
smoke, stub their butts
in the portico of Saint Mark's.

My feet among drink cans,
I stare out from the Balcony
to where a girl spits at her lover
in the centre of the Square.

They argue till wordless
inside a space filled with
pigeons and schoolchildren,
corn-sellers, spivs...

Lenses close in on forked
shadows, pearl walls;
the lagoon at midday
a mosaic of gold leaf.

11

One door leads in to another...
Baroque saints, fresh flowers,
votary candles askew, as if
pulled by different winds.

Crimson drapes frame the altar's
drama, ornate boxes set high.
With roof-windows open,
the church is preserving itself.

You are here to light candles,
ask for modest, essential things:
good heart, common sense,
a measure of hope.

But this is the land of opera!
Why don't you ask for something
extravagant, like an unselfish
lover, or one moment

when you stand, alive to
every petal and shadow,
your hand a glitter of dust motes
in stained-glass air.

    12
It would be good to have a painter
who knew everything about red –
                how it can lie hidden in rust or gold,
                hold multiplicities of rose.

It would be good to have a painter
who knew that red never goes away:
                first bud of spring; last leaf of autumn;
                winter-hard berry; summery hibiscus.

So shall I toast you, Titian,
in burgundy, claret, or rosé?
Now I am opening this peach-tinted grappa
which I should not have bought,
should not be drinking.

I raise a small measure
into the light that follows sunset.
Interesting! *Salute!*

13
On the one morning I am hungover
the police call. They want to know
when and where and why and what.

I offer dates, hypotheses,
false regrets for unsigned forms.
They juggle notebooks, words.

Fortunately, two half-languages
do not make a whole.
A far cry from inquisitive forbears,

they wear broad gold bands,
sport avuncular bellies. Concerned,
one points to my bare feet on marble.

The final week… Saturnine eyes
confer. What to do but shrug it off,
set shadowed jaws, leave?

14
The church is a maze of altars and angles
at any time, but today, Holy Saturday,
a massive Christ-on-the-Cross
slants through reshuffled pews.
Against the cavernous dark,
candles, electric and real.

With even his dog at a loss, a blind man
stumbles, displaces a woman in black.
Decades of piety have not prepared her for this:
she sidles away, unable to find the gesture.
The squat priest bends to his shoulder,
offering words' solidity.

15

Matteo's *nonna* pushes his pram over
cobbles, lifts it across stepped bridges,
singing his name and shouting,
'Piccolo bello! Piccolo bello!'

Matteo's eyelids have closed:
now he no longer hears,
but has begun to dream, her voice...
Hard work, being a baby in Italy.

16

Today, the peace summit.
In a gilded room, the President
talks and smiles beneath unseen
cobwebs woven by very old spiders.

His face to the sea, a monk
in saffron robes, white shirt,
prays for peace, on the Zattere.
His figured drum beats
soft-soft-loud-soft-loud.

A roar through ripples,
a well-aimed splash:
flushed triumph behind a wheel.

The monk gathers his things,
shifts ground, resumes his chant.
The sun is beginning to set.
People stroll past his back,
look out at gold light, gold water.

Lamplight

Glasshouses flash platinum-white against green hills —
one warmly intruded upon by setting sun
as though it held some radiant bloom which, opening
into dusk, glowed with all the day's spent energy.

Nearby, brown horses in a field... bodies you would think
impervious to light, haloed by an old gold haze
their eyes share in, offer the mystery of.

I watched in late winter, watched as gleaming tides
of sea-darkness flowed in — my breath
a mist I looked through, and the horses' breath
a further mist through which the sun,
surrendering, sank its bright ghost.

Later, the homeward drive, darkness
a settled thing, but for the streetlights —
cold, distinct, a counterpart of night:
with them, no yielding, softening,
as in the breath of lamplight with its hazy edge:
a humming corridor between brightness, void.

Winter Solstice

Unlocking the door most evenings now
I look up and see the stream of headlamps
flash along rain-fringed guttering –
light sped through a tremulous blackness.

Today, after long rain, the sky's a clear ice-grey,
my window a screen of liquid stars.
The sun flares as it falls behind the amber sill,
a curved shard tilting deep into my eyes.

The raindrops fill with flame, but hold – their solid
gleam now crescented by darkness.
When night comes, the room's a bright shape
on the pane, its door an opening into blackness.

Later, moonlight will tunnel a path through
the skylight, infusing the gloom of the alcove
where I sleep...
              I shall, perhaps, lie waking
as the small hours build steps towards day,

half-sensing the light, the dark, press against
each other, take shape inside each other –
reaching even to the dreamspaces
through which I float, and the depths
                       where moonstones grow.

Longcase Clock

In the farmhouse parlour for unmeasured years
in silence, a presence without reverberation.

Hefty, magisterial, its chimes once reached
the furthest corners of all rooms, stirred hardened dust,

each half-hour marked by a note waveringly clear
as a tuning fork's — tingling the flesh of wax-honeyed pine.

The clock casts the warm shadow of household god, familiar;
laid flat, it is roughly the length that will carry us out

into silence. How comforting it would be
to pull the case-door open and, in that cool space,

draw the chains slowly through your fingers,
instil a rhythm that could gauge time's oceanic sift

through hourglass waves.
                        Four gilded shells frame the dial;
under the single hand, a plant of strawberries ripens.

Behind the cracked parchment of its face, the clock waits
like a polite guest who would speak, but only

at the right moment, into a perfect silence.

Feeding the Birds

They wait in the trees for her, morning and evening —
doves mostly, with speckled torque on neck,
and sparrows, lighter than air, sporting plumage
of moccha, latte-beige. Our guest — an unclipped
bantam — dips as if crossing waves
in her body-boat of muscled snow:
even the small-brained have their sublime touches —
a lemon phosphorescence on cheeks, old gold
beak, red jelly dewlaps and coiffure.
The magpies' imperium scatters the rest
like flung seeds, near where sunflowers tower
and my mother stands — with our garden,
brought back from wildness, growing around her,
holding her in its open embrace.

Before the Heat

In the dawn wind, letting it travel through
my body, transport me with freshened sight
to here. I pluck weeds, skirt the pumpkin vine
ramping out from the young apple tree,
tapping its strength. A door slams. Inside I find
my mother still beautifully asleep
lying fish-shaped across her bed, wrapped in
a beach towel the greens of algae and leaf;
deep in her hip-bone, the infection
we live to outwit. On her table, a touch lamp:
light answerable to fingertips.
All night, windows streamed with cool air.
I'll soon shroud them ritually, draw up the moat bridge,
seal us inside this peace we have made.

Breath

Sleeplessness. At dawn, soft rain, the birds,
and music – Pachelbel's Canon played
over and over to soothe a mind still fazed
after a dizzy waking at one a.m. –
an alarm call to check on my mother.
With practised silence I opened her door,
in the quarter light leaned towards her face,
porcelain-pale, the strength of those fine bones,
to hear a breath. The same life-tide that swept us
apart has brought us to this grateful,
elegaic love, the hub we turn on –
Demeter and Kore becoming
each other, held in a graced affinity
between loss and loss. Twilight summer.

Lullaby

For Kyle

May nothing and no-one be a cage to you
while you sleep or when you wake –
not sleep itself, not dark, not light, not fear
not any of us sitting out here
hoping you will fall and settle like a feather
into sleep, not needing our eloquence
to convince, our cunning to outwit you.

May your journey through dreams
be that of a young hero, uprighting himself
after each fall, not suspecting yet
the dragons behind rocks, nor the power
he carries in that small casket
slung across his breast – containing sorrow,
love and hope, magically concentrated.

May you hear through your sleep the birds
at dawn, but not be woken by them.
Their songs, like their flight, connect earth
with air, air with water, but cannot
express the fourth quadrant, fire. The rising sun
lighting their wings is fire,
bringing warmth, and the beginning of shadow.
From shaken wings, a bright dew falls.

the world as poem

Diver

Toes ridging earth, landlocked.
     The river hardens its icy sheen
          that you must break. *Now*.

Beneath the splash, cold floods you
     till it is a pool of heat
          pulsing at the skull's base.

You are a bubble of panic,
     the weight inside you
          growing more leaden.

Then you reach, spin, thrust –
     the body claiming space
          in an expanse where

it is only a ripple.
     The rhythm of the breaths
          not taken

begins to beat through you;
     voiceless, you mouth
          small pearls of air,

ascend in a slow arc.
     Dragged by lightness
          you recross the surface:

the memory of drowning,
     a springboard
          to make you fly.

Night Walk

My own prints will lead me back.
I measure them, just to be sure...
Day's last wave has crashed,
the surfers cruised in, shining and black
under that jewelled band of red.
In the half-light, each wave is a shadow
broken on its shadow then released
into this white that seems to hold the day.

Whale-shaped, the headland concentrates
all depths, reaches, of grey; like a star,
the lighthouse with its slow subliminal wink.
The cliffs grow taller as I forge a path
between the sinking footprints and exploding surf —
lost, not yet frightened, whistling in the soft dark.

Headland

Barwon Heads, 1986

The tide is coming in as the day ebbs.
This is the moment to edge and clamber round
the cliff face I have seen from many angles,
never touched. My feet lock or slide on rocks
wet with the sky's gleam; my hands grip studs of quartz,
move over clay woven with funnel webs
bright with spray – inside each spiral
a cramped blackness fed by the sea.

Where the cliff becomes sheer, I descend
to the narrow shore, breathe between rocks
and sea mist; the river now in sight.
Climbing boulders slippery with moss,
my body still pays out its small thread of fear;
centres on effort, steadily, patiently.

Wind-Walking

Out of the house and into the wind.
Sand assaults skin with needlepoint stings,
rims half-closed eyes. I keep to the path
as my scarf pulls away, my hair knots.
To the wind my message is always the same:
I refuse to be annihilated, I refuse to be lulled.

From the cliffs I watch each headlong edge
scatter glass seeds onto sliding furrows.
Rebounding from rock, one wave hurtles
against another: above gritty swells
a fountain lifts to its flowering moment.
I walk, braced by the onrush, the cuttingly
soft voices, of wind, of water.

Time

I watch time pass in the dip and bounce
of branches, the spiral dance of my stripling
eucalyptus. Outside, I enter the pressure
and pull of it, my ten thousand footprints
mark sand as the river ruffles to fish-scaled
silver, and waves leave the ocean beach
scalloped with fine piping.
                    So much work to be done –
patterning, obliterating.

Can I breathe time as I breathe the wind,
draw its strength into my lungs, resist
its strength with my body? Today, this is not
gale-force time: we are evenly matched.
And I have known a sunlit freedom from time
when, not touching me, it listened, waited.

Skywriting

Winter Solstice, 1988

Someone has split this sunlit sky in half,
trailing a white streak that begins to fade
soon after the insistent buzz that made it.
Resoundingly, ocean writes on itself
thick lines that slide towards foam on jade –
illumined cyphers in a dissolving script.

On the shore I weave a path around
amulets, each with its story layered
in colour. As far as my eye can see,
jellyfish gleam from dry sand – small moons
sinking, hardening, becoming glass
punctuation marks among scrawls of seaweed.
Sealed off from this warm air, they lie exposed,
unknowing, dying of light.

Garden and Sea

New Year's Eve, 1986

On this day, summer will open its hands.
First, there is rain. The birds sing more freshly
after it, building high cities of notes.
Whole constellations of plums hover,
or lie with gashed redness, stillborn paleness.
Magpies swoop through the trees – benign;
close above our heads, as if we were
rooted in this waiting, growing place.

Later the waves rush, shining with olive darkness.
I circle and flow into new spaces
of coldness, new fathoms of blood.
In warm cradles of sand we rest, stripped
of old selves, till we are the children we tend –
running in play towards a brimming horizon.

Summer's End

No dolphins that night. The estuary
around me, then falling away as I
stepped, in a skin of light, shorewards
to witness clouds from a furnace-heart;
the sun, a meteorite in slow motion,
a drop of mercury on phosphorous.

The child's hand placed absently, trustingly,
on my thigh for a long minute as we stood
in half-dream, till his mother claimed him
with laughter, the boy too small for embarrassment,
the sun now a meniscus, but plotting
fireworks after its drowning — to tell us
with triumph, as heat turns to silence,
that summer is over.

Bathers at an Estuary

For my mother

Under the blue heat of a day between
summer and autumn, we waded through strands
of warmth and coolness weaving around us,
through us, entered that silken flow
to drift, our hands trawling the riverbed.
Sand crumbled from the banks, our horizon
the breaker closest to shore.
                                    The tide's pulse-beat
quickened as we shaped our movements
with and against the current's force,
each new pressure to be encompassed, or defied.
At last, you walked refreshed from the river
to lie beside my father, under the blue heat
while I stayed on, circling like a minnow,
edging towards the cradling, uncradling, sea.

Poem of Thanksgiving

On my father's recovery from illness

1

Clay river turning gold...

The risen moon has set its seal
on day's open blue letter.

Pebbles are sun-husked, scattered
coin, the melaleuca glows

with a honeyed flame above
obdurate green shadow.

Smooth trunks slide sinewy
into darkness. Smoke billows

over scrubland — mauve, then grey.

2

Curtains bell into the room
on eddies of evening freshness...

Crowded as goslings in a nest,
the freesias sprout from
their earthen chalice;

white inlaid with gold
but slowly browning
like the room, our faces...

Tides from an unknown sea
pluck at us, whisper endings
we cannot yet grasp.

3
Their cries with a beaked
sharpness, pierce the air;

rain slides from clouds broken
by sea winds tearing in;

flung backwards as they fall,
waves split, fly out into darkness;

a band of mist, bright as a corona,
rims the onrushing tide.

4
Lantern cloud, moon-flesh...

Pier shadows flap –
black sheets on a windy line.

Wings over water;
the night-flare of barium.

5
At first light, the first bird – a myna.

Window-framed, the vine's proscenium
ushers in the nervous dance of head and body
rehearsing to some hidden score.

Then, above the wind's slow swell,
staccato chortlings unlock
a savage carol that ends
in an exultant stillness.

6

The grasses are rose-tipped, dying.

Sunlight unrobes and bathes the river's body.
Colours, like lures, rising.

At the river mouth, crystal scales
lap on glinting ochre; the bridge casts

its shadow-line between fresh water, salt;
the stone flesh of headland looms,

pummelled by acres of air.
Sea birds, free from the self's dream,

our earth-rooted heaviness,
open/close wings as steadily as hearts, then –

poised, aslant – ride like leaves
the willed sea wind.

7

Water haemorrhages to whiteness.
Ocean shines with the living greenness of an eye.

Patterns cut and merge beneath flying riffs of surf:
alchemy of green into blue, wave into salt-fine mist.

Throughout this day,
perfect definition of line and essence,
as if wind had blown light
to a bell-like clearness.

Day's infinite depth
open and fluted like a shell.

8

An ibis steps
with uncanny elegance
into its shadow,
tests sand with claw,
beak-probes,
in flickering
slow motion:
touch and being,
stillness and seeking,
one: the ibis
stalks its image,
now white,
now grey,
on brimming glass.

9

Winter plantings: seeds of sound
thrust into the wind's furrow,
its hard, cool breath haloed by whisperings
of the never-born, the early-dead.

Leaning, the thrush opens its body,
sings… All gifts fulfilled in their
yielding up – to rhythms of light and air,
to an unknown music heard only
through these clear notes resounding
like the silver echo of a body.

10

On the table, cinerarias
purple and white:
fresh picked and perfect
in their velvet stillness.
Beyond us, the sea unrolls,
its daytime murmur softer
than the night's.

So often we feel the pattern, the pulse,
only as the wave breaks, or after it has broken.

But we have been given time,
may live in new ways towards each other.

We move about the house,
hearing, as in the sea's fall,
a steady breathing encompassing the breaking.

The flowers glow. Not yet
the hourglass journey
into no-being, new being.

A yellow ash circles the vase,
blends with the grained wood.

    11
One leaves some worlds
only to enter others.

As so often before, my eyes follow
black swans risen from the marshes,
turning in flight to shimmering points
then disappearing... Where?

Later, low gulls crest the sun's
last warmth, a surfer tilts and swoops
as if in flight.
                Powering shining breasts,
the grey wings row, unlit.

12

So many tides have brought us to this spring.
I stand on the pier and watch the bridge lights
tremble their beads of amber on jet satin.
Planks creak, almost companionable.
The heavy freshness of salt and blossom on air,
without bird sound, but crowded with
summer's promise. The wind barely breathes
in a haloed silence where tragedies, joys,
meet and enfold each other. Ocean's musk smell
still lingers inside the jasmine.
                              I will close the gate
and walk from the soft dark into the warm house,
and sit, waiting, remembering.

To the Estuary

An unpeopled shore. The river bares
the pale gold stretch that was a cricket pitch
last week. Under the pier, an inky pool
whose curved warmth I could lie in.
At the mouth I step on rock after rock
to where a channel of chased steel cuts,
to a crumbling ledge, the further shore.

My feet learn the riverbed, its crests
and gulleys; a map of vanished tides. The shore gleams,
turned by soldier crabs into a garment
of seed pearls, intricate as a night sky.
Prised from the estuary's heart, these pebbles
bear the same olive-emerald as its rocks —
whose stacked mussels glint in this tideless hour.

Pier

My place: to the right of the L-shaped pier,
wherever the water is breast-high. I've walked
against the wind's edges, warmed myself;
stepping into lime-cordial green
I nerve myself too, aware the sea must
throw me a surprise sometime; but not today...

Seaweed bobs and torpedos past — benign
dream-fragments. A dark mass I wade towards
is suddenly out beyond the pier, then gone:
that rippling dance sweeping it further
upriver in this perilous tide.
A short swim under wind-burnished clouds;
before leaving, I too bask in the spot
chosen by the shy, elegant manta.

Headland

Like stone, the body carries at its core,
in its textures, a history of becoming
and erosion. Here, limestone covers
dark silt from volcanos; there, scar tissue
of the intolerable: fissured rock-plates.
Time eats deeper into some lesions;
others fill with the detritus of life –
barnacled bones, void mussels and eggs –

or life itself: the spray-soaked, singing nest,
a bronze-eyed skink, clams winking at the sun
while keeping their counsel. The wind
strips clean the skin of rocks; scours flesh.
The sea, too, is theft and gift and fusion,
its cliffs storeyed with aeons of drowning, spawning.

Wathaurong Ceremony

The Barwon Bluff area, at the head of the Barwon River, was, and is, a place
of great significance for the Wathaurong people of the region. A large paved
area near the Barwon Heads bridge honours them, and presents configurations
in stone of the surrounding landforms and seascape.

Summer and autumn have mingled, gone their
separate ways. On a chill Sunday morning
we gaze at black, ochre and red stonework:
the Spit and estuary in miniature;
a mosaic of whale, eel, and mulloway
over the floor of this gathering place.

Far, it seems, from incalculable harm,
we sit on planed eucalypt to hear these words:
The earth is our mother, the river heals us.
Some prayers, Marcia gives us a song;
the children are still, with dreaming eyes.
In this small town, a beginning.
The shoreline's spill of cloud vanishes in sand,
is remade, mirror-clear.

Autumn

Yesterday's full moon possessed and drained
my psyche. I woke to a midnight sea
folding in on itself with hushed violence;
some unresolved memory pulsing through blood.
My print-weary eyes scanned a ghost story;
I let my dreams do their work without me.

Under today's dome of heat, I swim fast
to keep flush with the shore's cypress; the pier's
deconstructed shadow flows towards me.
The cold I dread has become a pleasure —
body, and essence, merged in one sensation.
The sun, part-screened by cloud, casts a faint
sparkle on ultramarine.
                              I dress slowly,
still breathless, at home in the spellbound light.

Eye

An eye as big as a fist looks up at me
from the river; small waves, veined with light,
sweep over the dented green iris.
At the eye's outer corner: glutinous folds
as of some *prima materia.*
The white of the eye absorbs the naked sky.
The image tilts and sways – a photograph
developing inside an olive wash.

I lie on warm sand. This time, my angled glasses
wear what they refract: in the darkroom
beneath my hat, the flesh round my eye is writ large,
pouched and pore-pocked; the iris, blue-black satin.
Lashes are thorn-sharp reeds rimming a pool;
the eye's white has become a tiny beach.

The Wind

A river vehemently seabound. Fatigue
made me sway in the wind, I could not hold
the moment in focus. A space opened
as one kind of seeing lapsed, and I flowed,
a minute part of everything – then glimpsed
my own absence from all this process and
particularity: the world as poem.

As if hearing my thoughts, the wind argued
and cajoled, its body enveloped mine,
cold hands unshaped me – so that I entered
a limitless nothingness. Sky and sea
sped backwards, sped away, as it blew me
home bearing a capsule of death, a seed
of acceptance for my burial garden.

Winter Solstice

Later, little claws of rain will scratch at
headlights as I walk home. Now, my body
shaken by each car on the bridge, I watch
the many-voiced flow that has become
a locus of existence, a devotion:
my life so small a thing before such power –
while so reverberant itself, I can feel
and name the state of light on skeined contours;
net, for others to consume, a fish-poem
that carries the river's taste in its flesh.
I drink the silence, eavesdropping on what
dusk and daylight have to say to each other,
the rain still soft – silk loosed from air's cocoon –
the first stutter of car beams skimming the river.

Winter Sunset

What is it about two fishermen
in a flat-bottomed boat at rest upon
crushed petals of pink, ice-blue, crimson?
The sense of solitary communion
doubled, they make a small statement within
this metamorphosis: wild, yet serene.
Between tides, the river moves both ways,
unzipped along the middle by the nose
and tailfin of a young seal on its own quest –
wide eddies like wings behind it.
I recall the noonday scene, missed by those
wordless philosophers – rays from a white
sun suffusing clouds, trees, and houses,
become mist; the flow tide stilled by light.

Upstream

Light chevrons calm water; a shirtless
canoeist wears the morning on his back,
drops firing the air as his paddle arcs.
I have tracked the river to where the mangroves
take hold and the bird-life gets serious –
a kingfisher, totemic on a pole;
pelicans cruising low – three wing-beats
then a glide; ibis gathered in a field
as if on a contemplative picnic.
In reedy nooks, lone fishermen dream up
hot dinners. I skirt their silence while
preserving my own, which grows more spacious
the further I move from cars, lawnmowers, dogs;
builds into an airy shell.

Estuary

Seahorse clouds, a fingernail's curve
of moon. I wade through green swathes, as if
reclaiming pieces of memory; as if
my brain were reconstituting itself —
cell by cell, rebuilding rooms; unlocking
others, long-sealed, to let this sea light flow through.

My feet step from slurred prints, body tensing
before each wave with its rags of seaweed,
unseen flurries — sometimes a fleeting sting.
Out on the beach, the sky's a jigsaw this new tide
will fill in; spread with a silver-blue cloth.
Between low rocks, slash and eruption,
upsurge of chimerical white, chalices
of cloudless jade stilled to translucence.

Summer

A northerly holds sway on this
hottest day for years, sand ghosting the damp verge,
a gritty coating on oiled skin. I look out
past shirred crystal to leaf-green, cerulean;
wade in, wanting to be braced by chill pressures,
until the breakers I stand beyond, arch back:
sudden tears from parched blue. My eyes salt-stung,
I swim where waves sheer off to meet the river.

Now, near day's end, I lie in these
liquid inches as if earthed in ocean;
the sun still dangerous on my eyelids.
But, swathed by gold light, here I stay —
letting thoughts evaporate,
thirsting for fresh beginnings.

Mist

Earth breath, flower breath, tree breath... The river itself
a matter of belief, phantom birds arrowing
through veils of nothingness. Up on the cliffs:
the light is metallic, unstable, as in
an old film; the sun's pollined heart stays trapped
behind petals of cloud. Waves fountain,
cirrus-backed, as if white were inside
everything, and mist deeper inside that white.

The horizon appears – an unwalked path
beyond a grey sea mazed with prints of light.
Clouds bloom, the day opens its window wide,
lets the steam out. A heron peers from a rail,
at its beak's tip a drop of salt water
that globes this sun-filled moment.

Ocean

Life rolls towards you, giving and breaking. You hear:
grief-cries, hunger's anger, despair's numb crash.
A torn whisper conjures the ghosts of chance.
Longing flowers inside its lapse, white
foliage rustles... Sighs from a cloud throat –
beyond fear, beyond rapture. You hear:
the angelic hiss of dreams; gossip,
rumours of war, Babel. The glint of blades
as waves tilt down, yield to a singing vapour –
voice of the one and the many. You hear:
the sound of a million ripped temple veils;
the sound of a field of light harvesting itself;
the first sound and the last, both conjoined;
a sound curved as the Tao.

Tides

Silent as virtue, the tide enters the coast —
holding back at first, a grateful guest,
then assuredly at home, ready to bring
its whole life swiftly in. As with bird flight —
always a new concordance of darkness, light,
as they split and meld, fertilise each other.

At ebb tide, scuffed waves circle the stream's centre,
push back to where long breakers tip,
hook down on mirrors slick with sun.
Clouds mass, tumble, in a fast sky; ibis sway
on thermals, hierophants of a primal peace —
the lilt of their languorous black wings
a footnote in the unwritten book of days;
part of the tremendous drift of things.

Sea Pool

Here in this vessel of warmed brine, to bathe
and float myself into serenity.
At eye level an ibis forages
close-by, leaves off to practise stillness as if
waiting for life's next gift to manifest,
intimate with this place, moment: sluiced rocks,
tail-ruffling wind, solstice sun.

Set in a Venetian mask with dark pronged bill:
obsidian eyes. Off-white plumage,
unbeautiful till its hidden life
fans into myth – a sculptured fugue ripples
above the coastline; a cloak of power worn
as simply as stillness, then folded close
while the ibis again probes sea-scarred basalt.

Heat

At night, the sound of rain falling upwards,
a resonance like untapped memory,
till dawn plants bird voices in soft thunder.
By day, the coast sequestered behind blue mist,
a platinum slick rides each wave. I crouch
where pools of cold flood the shallows' warmth
to watch terns on a row of rocks: black-capped
sentinels facing out to sea —
forked tails and wing-tips spiking air, as they groom.
The tide floods the rocks; an eye-blink switch
from squatness to wide-winged, virtuosic flair
scything a path over the estuary.
Clouds thin to air, the heat pulses more fiercely,
new energy rolls into the river.

Acknowledgements

Poems have appeared previously in *Voices from the Honeycomb* (Jacaranda: Brisbane, 1986), *Metamorphoses* (Dangaroo: Sydney, 1988), *Turning the Hourglass* (Dangaroo: Sydney, 1990), *Mayflies in Amber* (A&R/HarperCollins: Sydney, 1993), *The Body in Time* (Spinifex: Melbourne, 1995), *Listening to a Far Sea* (Hale & Iremonger: Sydney, 1998), *The Sixth Swan* (Five Islands Press: Wollongong, 2001), *Sea Wall and River Light* (Five Islands Press: Melbourne, 2006), and *The Mystery of Rosa Morland* (Clouds of Magellan: Melbourne, 2008).

Some of the uncollected poems in this book have appeared in *The Age*, *The Australian*, *Australian Book Review*, *Australian Nationalism Reconsidered*, ed. Adi Wimmer (Stauffenburg Verlag: Tübingen, 1999), *The Best Australian Poems 2004*, ed. Les Murray (Black Inc.: Melbourne, 2006), *Blue Dog*, *The Canberra Times*, *Critical Survey* (UK), *Eclogues: the Newcastle Poetry Anthology 2007*, ed. Martin Harrison, John Jenkins and Jan Owen, *Eureka Street* (online journal), *Landbridge: Contemporary Australian Poetry*, ed. John Kinsella (Fremantle Arts Centre Press: Fremantle, 1999), *Poetry* (Chicago), *Poetry Ireland Review*, *Sunweight: the Newcastle Poetry Prize Anthology 2005*, ed. Judith Beveridge and Judy Johnson, *The Paradise Anthology, issue 4*, ed. Michael Crane, *Voices* (National Library of Australia), *Westerly*, and *Zeitschrift für Australienstudien, issue 24*, 2010 (online journal, University of Klagenfurt).

A number of poems appear in revised versions.

To the friends who have shared the journey of poetry with me, offering their wisdom, enthusiasm and support, I offer my grateful appreciation.

My special thanks to Rosemary Blake, Sandy Fitts, Katherine Gallagher, and Joel Magarey; and to Angela Livingstone and Linda Saunders.

And my cordial thanks to my publisher, David Musgrave; and to Matthew Holt for his cover design.

Sources of Poems

Small Wonders
Voices from the Honeycomb: Late Summer Garden, Red Admirals in Shropshire.
Mayflies in Amber: All poems from Dragonfly to Mayfly.
Sea Wall and River Light: Albatrosses, The Parliament of Birds, Pelicans, The Ibis Grove, Weedy Seadragons, Starfish.
Uncollected: Terns, Air, Solo, At the Cliffs, What Herons Know, Owl, Wedge-Tailed Eagle, Tawny Frogmouths, Lyrebirds, Cockatoos at Dawn, Macaws, Small Wonders, The Hummingbird Suite, In Praise of Seahorses, Leafy Seadragons, Wolf-Fish, Pearly Nautilus.

The Wing Collection
Voices from the Honeycomb: Dürer's *The Little Owl*, Sparrows, Wings, The Annunciation, Flyers, Birdcage.
Turning the Hourglass: Remembering Ophelia, Dracula, Assignation, Sower.
The Body in Time: Primal Scene, Assemblage.
The Mystery of Rosa Morland: Seamus L'Estrange: Spirit Photographer.
Uncollected: Angels: a Dossier, Doll Writer, Walpurgisnacht, Last Scene, The Collector, Litany.

The Gold Honeycomb
Metamorphoses: All poems from Philomela to Underworld.
Listening to a Far Sea: All poems from Orpheus in the Underworld to Nike.

The Sixth Swan
All poems are from *The Sixth Swan.*

Secret Lives

Voices from the Honeycomb: Lamplight, Longcase Clock, Lullaby.
Turning the Hourglass: In Conversation, Dressmaker, Hourglass in an Interior, The Chinese Astronomer, Travelling Alone, Winter Solstice.
The Body in Time: Rooms, In the House, Wind, Accident, Night Driving, Venice Notebook.
Uncollected: The Power of Mirrors, Feeding the Birds, Before the Heat, Breath.

The World as Poem

Voices from the Honeycomb: Diver, Night Walk.
Turning the Hourglass: Headland: *Barwon Heads, 1986*, Wind-Walking, Time, Skywriting, Garden and Sea, Bathers at an Estuary, Poem of Thanksgiving.
The Body in Time: Summer's End.
Sea Wall and River Light: All poems from To the Estuary to Heat.

Notes

Poems in *The Gold Honeycomb* section draw upon versions of Greek myths from a wide range of sources, of which Homer's *The Iliad,* Euripides' *Trojan Women,* and Ovid's *Metamorphoses,* are the most important. Robert Graves' *The Greek Myths,* and various dictionaries of Greek mythology, were also used. The poems in *The Sixth Swan* are based on stories from *Grimms' Fairy Tales.* 'The Frog Prince' is usually translated as 'The Frog King'. 'The Prince and the Princess' is usually titled 'The Two Kings' Children'. The individual fairy stories can be found on various sites on the internet, along with information regarding Greek myths, and information about the birds, insects, and sea creatures of *Small Wonders.*

All of the bird poems, except for Owl, Lyrebirds, Cockatoos at Dawn, Macaws, Small Wonders, and The Hummingbird Suite, were based on bird life observed in and around Barwon Heads, a town on the southeast coast of Victoria. All the poems in *The World as Poem* were written at Barwon Heads, except for Wind-Walking, Time, Skywriting, Garden and Sea, Summer's End, and Bathers at an Estuary, which were written at Port Noarlunga South, South Australia.

p.18   At the Cliffs: 'red-cap' refers to the red-capped plover.

p.24   Owl: The starting point of this poem was some filmed footage of owlets in their nest, in a nature documentary.

p.32   The Hummingbird Suite: The quote from Emily Dickinson in Hummingbird Questions is from The Wind – tapped like a tired Man; that from Mary Oliver in Hummingbird Soul is from Long Afternoon at the Edge of Little Sister Pond.

p.54   Bees: 'At Aphrodite's shrine on Mount Eryx a golden honeycomb was displayed, said to have been a votive offering presented by Daedalus when he fled to Sicily.' Robert Graves, *The Greek Myths,* 18.3.

p.56   Bee Flies: In Greek mythology, Aristaeus, a bee-keeper, was punished after his pursuit of Eurydice led to her death by snakebite: all his bees were killed by her sister Dryads. Finally he is said to have obtained new swarms of bees from the carcases of bulls; these bees are thought to have been, in fact, bee flies.

p.63 Fireflies: In various places in Malaysia, Indonesia and the Philippines, night river tours take travellers past trees lit by fireflies.

p.64 Mayfly: Mayfly nymphs moult many times in the aquatic stage; then they float to the surface and become winged subimagos resembling the adult, before a final moult into the adult. Mayflies are the only insects where a winged form undergoes moulting.

p.69 Wings: One key painting referred to is 'Three Hovering Angels' by the Master of the Housebook ('Drei schwebende Engel' by Meister des Hausbuchs); other influences are from images in 'The Mirror of Salvation Altarpiece in Basel' by Konrad Witz.

p.76 Praise: Information regarding microscopic engraving on hair can be found on various websites, including www.chinaculture.org

p.78 Flyers: *Light Years Away* won the Grand Prix at the 1981 Cannes Film Festival. In it, twenty-year-old Jonas meets Yoshka, a man in his fifties, who is building a flying machine: he says he has been given special knowledge by the birds, and taught how to fly. Yoshka gives Jonas a difficult time as he tests him so as to induct him into his secrets, then takes off on his constructed wings; this leads to his death.

p.81 Doll Writer: In 1928, an automaton was donated to the Franklin Institute, Philadelphia. Delivered in pieces, it had almost been ruined in a fire many years before. When repaired it produced three poems and four drawings, and inscribed the name of its maker, Henri Maillardet. Displayed for decades in eighteenth-century woman's clothing, it now wears male attire. Information regarding the Franklin Institute's Automaton can be found on its website.

p.90 Walpurgisnacht: As St Walburga was canonised on May 1st, her name became associated in many European countries with celebrations on the eve of May Day. In Germany, witches were believed to hold revels on the Brochen mountain on Walpurgis Night – a time therefore also associated with dark forces and the uncanny.

p.96 The Collector: The starting point of this poem was the following notice in the *International Herald Tribune*, 12.12.1997: 'Angel Wings. $89.95 plus shipping and handling from The Pyramid Collection, Altid Park, P.O. Box 3333, Chelmsford, Massachusetts, 01824.'

p.100 Sower: In *The Man Who Planted Trees*, Jean Giono tells the (fictional) story of a shepherd who, after the deaths of his wife and child, devoted his life to planting acorns in a desolate area in France. Forests grew, and the landscape was reclaimed. The Parable of the Sower, told in Luke 8:5, describes the dropping of seeds on a path, on rocky ground, and on thorns; but the seeds that fell on good earth grew, yielding abundantly. In ancient Greece, the oak groves surrounding the temple of Zeus at Dodona were thought to be endowed with a gift of prophecy, and the sound of their leaves interpreted as oracles.

p.103 Philomela: Raped by her brother-in-law, who cut out her tongue, and imprisoned her, Philomela wove a tapestry which told the story, and had it sent to her sister. A terrible revenge followed, after which Philomela was changed into a nightingale.

p.104 Scylla, Daughter of Nisus: Scylla fell in love with King Minos when he was attacking her father's kingdom. She cut a lock of her father's hair, on which his power depended, and gave it to Minos who then defeated him. Scylla was transformed into a ciris bird – now unknown – when she drowned after being attacked by her father, in the form of a sea-eagle.

pp.106-111 Andromache, Hecabe, Astyanax, Cassandra, and Helen, all feature in *The Iliad.*

p.113 The Pool: The story of Echo, a nymph who was in love with, but spurned by, Narcissus, lover of his own reflection, is told by Ovid. Punished by Hera for a small offence, she could only repeat the final syllables of another person's speech.

p.117 Weaver: Arachne, a young Lydian woman, was a weaver whose skill proved a match for that of the goddess Athena, in a contest held between them. Infuriated, Athena beat her rival with a shuttle; because of the pain she endured, Arachne hanged herself. But, though she was then changed into a spider by Athena in a further act of vengeance, Arachne's gift for spinning continued unimpaired.

p.118 Demeter: An ancient mother-goddess, and goddess of fertility. Her daughter Persephone (also known as Kore, 'the Maiden') was carried off by Hades, who ruled the Underworld. Enraged, and in grief, Demeter wandered over the earth, but was reconciled when Persephone could return to earth during spring and summer. This myth is thought to dramatise the cycle of the seasons, and the mystery of renewal following winter's dearth.

p.120 Orpheus in the Underworld: Orpheus's lyre playing and singing were said to charm wild animals and cause stones and trees to follow the sound of his music. When his wife Eurydice died, he descended to the Underworld and played so movingly that Hades freed her to return to earth with Orpheus – on condition that he not look back until Eurydice reached the light of the sun.

p.121 Arion: The quotation is from *Dictionary of Classical Mythology,* by Edward Tripp.

p.122 Daedalus: The quotation is from Robert Graves' *The Greek Myths.* See also the entry for 'Bees'.

p.127 Atlas: One of the gigantic Titans, he held up the sky, keeping it separate from the earth. He was associated in ancient times with what is now known as the Grand Atlas Range, in eastern and southern Morocco. One story tells of his being turned into a mountain by Perseus.

p.128 Teiresias: A seer who, after striking two coupling snakes with his staff, was transformed into a woman for part of his life, and returned to his masculine form after meeting, and striking, two more snakes coupling. He was later blinded by the Goddess Hera.

p.131 Typhon: A monster who had a hundred burning snake heads and spoke with the voices of men and animals. He tried to overthrow the gods and rule the universe. Zeus fought him and eventually prevailed.

p.132 Menagerie: Circe, a sorceress, lived on the island of Aeaea, and was adept at transforming men and women into beasts. She features in *The Odyssey.*

p.133 The Graeae: Grey-haired from birth, they were called the Graeae, 'Grey Women'. They had only one eye and one tooth between them; these were stolen by Perseus.

p.134 Oracle: The Delphic Oracle was the most important oracle in ancient Greece. Prophecies were voiced by the Pythia, who sat on a tripod, in a state of trance.

p.152 Bearskin: After a war, a homeless young soldier came, in his wanderings, to a heath where he sat reflecting sadly on his fate as he knew about nothing but guns, and thought he must starve. A stranger with a cloven hoof and a green jacket appeared. He promised the young man money, but first wanted him to prove his courage. Suddenly a great bear appeared, which the soldier shot. The stranger was satisfied on that score, but said there was another condition. 'Just as long as it won't cost me my soul,' said the soldier, who knew with whom he was dealing. He would have to go seven years without washing, or cutting his hair or nails, he was told; and he must not say the Lord's Prayer. Should he die during that time, the devil would claim him; should he survive, he would be free and rich. The soldier agreed, then put on the green jacket which always had a handful of money in its pocket. He also had to wear the skin of the bear, which he was to sleep in, never using a bed...

p.156 Jorinda and Joringel: An old sorceress lived in a castle in the middle of a great forest. Any maiden who came near would be changed by her into a bird, and imprisoned; she had seven thousand such birds. Once, Jorinda and Joringel, a betrothed couple, were walking in the forest, not far from the castle. Dusk came, and they were filled with melancholy and foreboding. Jorinda was changed into a nightingale, while Joringel became rooted to the spot. The sorceress caught the nightingale, but Joringel was set free from his trance. One night, he dreamed of a blood-red flower, with a pearl in the middle: it had the power to set free whatever and whomever it touched. After nine days' searching he found this flower, and headed for the castle. There the enchanted maidens were freed by its touch.

p.163 The Handless Maiden: A miller bartered his daughter to the devil who, when he came to take her, had no power over her, because of her virtue. Even when the miller cut off her hands, the devil could not take her. She wandered in the wilderness, then was found and married by a king, but later cast out because of the devil's intervention. She and her child stayed seven years in a cottage and were well cared for. By the grace of God and through her own piety, the hands that had been chopped off grew back again.

p.203 Breath: See entry for 'Demeter' above. 'Kore' is pronounced with two syllables.